MW01248325

"I have been greatly helped by Tony Merida's preaching and have been inspired by his friendship. The nine essentials Tony lays out in *Church Planter* are applicable to far more than leaders of the church of Jesus Christ; everyone would do well to ingest these lessons."

Dr. Bryan Loritts, Teaching Pastor, The Summit Church; Author, *The Offensive Church*

"*Church Planter: Nine Essentials for Being Faithful and Effective* by Tony Merida is a must-read for anyone serious about church planting. The combination of biblical truth and practical guidance stands out in the world of church-planting books. Tony provides both the inspiration and the tools necessary for planting faithful and effective, gospel-centered churches. As a church-planting professor, I highly recommend this book to all aspiring and current church planters who desire to faithfully serve God's mission."

George Ross, NAMB Church Planting and Ministry Center Director; Professor of Church Planting and Evangelism at NOBTS

"The coaching Tony Merida offers in *Church Planter* is solidly biblical and readily applicable. It's packed with practical wisdom for planters and their teams. Each chapter is worth visiting again and again, because no ministry leader will ever outgrow these truths. Every church planting team member will benefit from this book!"

Jen Oshman, Author; speaker; women's ministry director

"When I planted The Austin Stone in 2002, I would have given the world to have a resource like *Church Planter*. Tony Merida has written the go-to, all-encompassing manual for church-planting efficiency. The church has desperately needed a resource like Merida has delivered."

Matt Carter, VP of Mobilization for Send Network/NAMB

"If we want to see a gospel movement in North America, we must intentionally develop the next generation of church planters. Tony Merida's new book, *Church Planter: Nine Essentials for Being Faithful and Effective,* can play a critical part in preparing godly men who will be ready for the task ahead. I've seen Tony's work firsthand, and I know he is committed to training faithful, biblical leaders for Great Commission churches. As you and your church help equip church planters to pursue the Great Commission in North America and around the world, this book will be an essential resource!"

Kevin Ezell, President of the North American Mission Board

"If people around the world are going to hear the gospel proclaimed and grow in godliness, then we need sound leaders planting sound churches. And if the Lord has called you to participate in this essential work, then *Church Planter: Nine Essentials for Being Faithful and Effective* is the book you need to read. In his well-known winsome and wise way, Tony Merida not only provides you with practical tools, he reminds you to pursue Christ as you proclaim him, to rest in Christ as you labor for him, and to love Christ as you love his people."

Courtney Doctor, Director of Women's Initiatives, The Gospel Coalition; Bible teacher and author

"With his extensive experience planting a church-planting church and training hundreds of church planters, Tony Merida distills his pastoral wisdom and a wealth of church planting literature into nine essentials that every planter must consider. This book is an invaluable resource for equipping the next generation of church planters to be theologically sound, spiritually robust, and relationally healthy."

Walter R. Strickland II, PhD., Teaching Pastor Imago Dei Church; Theology Professor at Southeastern Baptist Theological Seminary

"Church planters who are effective but not pragmatic are rare gems in the Kingdom landscape. Tony is one such rare gem. This helpful resource flows straight out of his robust biblical convictions in ecclesiology and missiology, and delivers practical, cross-cultural directives for faithful and fruitful church planting. Every church planter and every partner for church planting will be served well by Tony's work."

Adam Bailie, Senior Lead Pastor, Christ Church

"Tony Merida's introduction to church planting is soaked in Scripture, laden with practical and pastoral advice, enriched by episodes and quotations from heroes of the faith, all in a highly accessible form. Tony touches on the great issues—calling, leadership, and relationships—and adds welcome commentary on a host of helpful topics, such as ambition, marriage, and exercise. The prompts for prayer and reflection make the book even more valuable."

Dan Doriani, Author and professor of theology at
Covenant Theological Seminary

"*Church Planter: Nine Essentials for Being Faithful and Effective* is a must-read for anyone passionate about the Great Commission. This book is biblically refreshing, practically accessible, and theologically driven. Tony Merida writes not only as a pastor and planter but also as a church planting network leader, theologian, and spiritual father. His wisdom is rich, complete, and Christ-exalting. Every chapter breathes grace and practical insight, making it an invaluable resource for those committed to building gospel-centered churches that glorify God."

Dr. Doug Logan, Jr., President of Grimké Seminary and
Dean of Grimké Urban; Author of *On the Block:
Developing a Biblical Picture for Missional Engagement*

"Tony Merida is one of my favorite preachers and authors as well as one of the most faithful church planters I know. In *Church Planter: Nine Essentials for Being Faithful and Effective*, Dr. Merida uses his considerable gifts and experience to produce this essential work for actual and potential church planters. I highly recommend *Church Planter* to every minister, especially those engaged in the work of church planting."

Jason K. Allen, Ph.D., President of Midwestern Baptist Theological Seminary & Spurgeon College

Church Planter

CHURCH PLANTER

Nine Essentials for Being
Faithful and Effective

TONY MERIDA

GCD Books

Church Planter: Nine Essentials for Being Faithful and Effective

© 2024 Tony Merida
All rights reserved.

GCD Books
Plymouth, MI

GCD Books is a ministry of Gospel-Centered Discipleship. Our purpose is to produce resources that make, mature, and multiply disciples of Jesus.

To get more resources from Gospel-Centered Discipleship, visit us at GCDiscipleship.com/books and follow us on X @GCDiscipleship.

GCD editorial: Vicki Bentley
Front cover design: Laura Schembre (copperstreetdesign.com)
Back cover & interior design: Benjamin Vrbicek

Paperback ISBN: 979-8-9889-2985-7
Ebook ISBN: 979-8-9889-2986-4

Unless otherwise noted Scripture quotations are from quotations are from The ESV® Bible (The Holy Bible, English Standard Version®), copyright © 2001 by Crossway, a publishing ministry of Good News Publishers. 2016 Text Edition. Used by permission. All rights reserved.

Contents

Acknowledgments

This book is the fruit of many partners in the gospel. I am indebted to Kevin Ezell, president of the North American Mission Board (NAMB), and to Vance Pitman, who leads NAMB's church-planting efforts as the president of Send Network, for the opportunity to serve in my current role. I still remember my first phone call with Vance about the possibility of joining the team. It came as a great surprise to me, and looking back now, I see it as God providentially opening a door for fruitful ministry. Kevin's passion for the gospel and love for church planters is refreshing to my soul. Vance's enthusiastic leadership, passion for the gospel, heart for cities and nations, devotion to prayer, and expositional preaching are just a handful of reasons why I admire him so much.

To Travis Ogle, Noah Oldham, Brian Bloye, Bryan Loritts, Matt Carter, and José Abella: it's a joy and privilege to labor with you, brothers. I feel as though the Lord has truly put us together for such a time as this. To Chad Childress and the Planter Development team, thank you for the joy of locking arms together as we prepare, assess, care for, and equip church planters. I pray that the Lord will give us many more years to serve our network together. To the leaders in the field at Send, thank you for your faithful labor as you seek to establish new churches across

North America. I have learned from many of you and look forward to knowing you better in the coming years.

To Christy Britton, my project manager, thank you. This book and many other projects would not be complete apart from your tireless and joyful labor.

I recognize that I stand on the shoulders of many leaders and church planters. Over the last decade, I have learned from many individuals across various church-planting networks and tribes. For instance, my time at Acts 29 was formative as I learned from gospel-centered leaders around the world. I still cherish many of these friendships and continue to support any movement of churches trying to advance the kingdom of God around the world.

To my elders at Imago Dei Church, I couldn't ask for a better council. Thank you for giving me the freedom to serve the broader church outside of IDC. It has been amazing to be part of a multiplying church sending people out all over the world for mission and church planting. Your support of my work at Send reflects your heart for church planting and the expansion of the kingdom.

To Jeremy Writebol, thank you for your willingness to publish my church-planting book before it ever took this final shape, my friend. After taking on this new role at Send, Jeremy and the folks at Gospel-Centered Discipleship allowed me to repurpose some of the content from my previous book *The Faithful Church Planter*, add to it, and give it a new structure and flow. The result is what I hope will be a very helpful resource on the essentials of a faithful and effective church planter.

To my bride, Kimberly, where would I be without you, my dear companion? I don't want to think about it. My love for you grows by the day. None of my work happens apart from your support and encouragement. Thank you for all the ways you have helped me and contributed to this book.

Most of all, I must thank Jesus, the sovereign Head of the church. Thank you for the cross and the empty tomb. Because you conquered death, we have something to preach and a mission that is not in vain. May you receive this little book as an offering of my worship to you, my King.

Foreword by Vance Pitman

Leadership matters. Always has, always will. Regardless of the generation, context, or domain, the world needs leaders. That is why I am thrilled that my friend and co-laborer, Tony Merida, has written this book outlining the type of leadership that is essential in church planting.

The Bible is filled with examples demonstrating the effect of good and not-so-good leaders. There is an interesting story in the Old Testament that took place early in the life of a leader we all know named David. Samuel, the prophet of God, was sent by the Lord to the house of Jesse the Bethlehemite to find and anoint a new king for Israel. When he arrived at Jesse's home, Samuel began to examine each of Jesse's sons to determine which of them had all the kingly qualities required for the job. One by one, Jesse paraded his sons in front of Samuel. He started with the strongest, bravest, and brightest, and worked his way down the list. When Samuel laid eyes on Eliab, the oldest and most obvious choice, he thought for sure he'd found his man. It was at that moment that God spoke to Samuel and gave him a profound word of wisdom, "Do not look on his appearance or on the height of his stature, because I have rejected him. For the LORD sees not as man sees; man looks on the outward appearance, but the Lord looks on the heart" (1 Sam. 16:7). The lesson from this story is simple: when it comes to spiritual leadership, God measures by a different standard.

For the past several decades, there has been an increased zeal for planting new churches in North America. Unfortunately, we've often looked for church-planting leaders the way Jesse and Samuel looked at Jesse's sons, settling for a standard far less than what God would demand in his Word.

Does the planter have experience?
Can the planter cast vision?
Is the planter a high-capacity leader?
Is the planter a dynamic communicator?

These (and others) are the types of questions often asked to determine the right leader when planting churches.

Don't misunderstand me. I'm not saying those things don't matter. I'm simply saying that those things by themselves do not capture the whole picture of what is needed to be a faithful and effective church planter.

Church planting is about the eternal redemptive mission of God. Church planting is about engaging cities with the gospel, reaching those far from God, and multiplying disciples. It's about the preaching and teaching of God's divinely inspired Word. It's born out of the overflow of an intimate love relationship with Jesus that spills into relationships with others locally and globally.

Church planting is a massive undertaking. It is engaging in a very real spiritual war on the front lines. It's about seeking to take back ground the enemy has claimed as his own territory through the truth of the gospel and the power of the Holy Spirit. For all these reasons and one thousand more, we must make certain that we are hearing clearly from the Lord in evaluating those who will be leading teams of men and women sent out to plant new churches.

In this book, Tony Merida masterfully captures what is being called the *Nine Essentials of Faithful and Effective Church Planters*. He writes as a practitioner and as an example for all of us.

Our team at Send Network has worked with Tony to try to discern from the pages of Scripture exactly what is required of those seeking to join in God's kingdom activity through multiplying disciples and churches. I believe the pages you are about to read capture the essence of what leadership looks like that qualifies a man to be a church planter. Does every planter need to have mastered every one of these essentials? Absolutely not. But these are qualities every planter sent out to lead a team should have present and growing in his life. These essentials should describe who he is and who he is becoming through his abiding relationship in Jesus.

I believe these nine essentials provide a target for the kind of leaders we are seeking to send out to plant churches. And I believe if we aim for this target, we have an opportunity to see a significant moment in our lifetime.

I do not believe we can create spiritual movement. I do believe, however, that if we obey the biblical principles of multiplying disciples and churches that pour out of the example of the early church, we are lifting our sails so that, should the wind of the Spirit of God choose to blow and create movement, we are ready to ride the wave of his activity. And like it did in Acts 13 with Paul and Barnabas, it begins with selecting leaders.

May we consider these nine essentials as we prayerfully discern who should be sent out as leaders in the mission. And may the Lord raise up a generation of faithful and effective church planters to see his kingdom expand locally and globally through the multiplication of disciples and churches!

I am thankful for my brother Tony and for this book to be a tool in the hands of church-planting leaders for generations to come.

Vance Pitman
Pastor, Author, and President of Send Network

Introduction

One of the joys of my ministry career has been training aspiring church planters around the world. For several years, I had the privilege of teaching church planters at Kyiv Theological Seminary in Ukraine for a week each year. The church-planting program was started by my friend, Joel, who had a vision for planting churches across the former Soviet Union. One of my favorite memories happened one year during student introductions and testimonies. A brother named Emmanuel, a massive man from Lithuania who had spent time in prison, shared about his rough former life. He said the only reason he had opened a Bible in those days was to use its pages to smoke various substances, but now he's opening the Bible to preach from it! How do you go from smoking the Bible to preaching the Bible? The only explanation is that Jesus Christ saves sinners (1 Tim. 1:15). Due to Christ's work in his heart, Emmanuel became a humble and gentle leader.

God can change the most hard-edged sinners, the vilest men and women, and turn them into ambassadors for Christ (2 Cor. 5:20). He changed Paul from a religious terrorist into a pioneer evangelist and church planter (Gal. 1:11–23), and God is still doing this transforming work today. Sure, we may not have spent time in prison, nor have a testimony exactly like Paul's.

Still, everyone's story is powerful because God has taken those who were spiritually dead and made us alive together with Christ (Eph. 2:1–9).

In conversations with strangers, the question often comes up: "So, what do you do?" I love to have them guess since they rarely choose "pastor." I then like to tell them, "I'm more surprised than you are!" The grace of God truly is stunning, and you never know from where the next great ministry leader may come. He may be a rebellious church kid right now, a freshman at the local college, the little hipster at the coffee shop, or the high school kid sneaking off campus to smoke e-cigs. Jesus Christ can take a mess of a person and turn them into a messenger of life. That's because the gospel still works. It is still the power of God unto salvation (Rom. 1:16). As church planters and ministry leaders, we must have an unshakable confidence in the gospel.

What Makes a Church Planter?

At Send Network, we have identified nine essential qualities of a faithful and effective church planter. While others have identified additional or differing traits, we have found these particular competencies to serve church plants and church-planting teams well.[1] This concise book is intended to offer a brief introduction to each one.

Some church planters will be stronger in some areas than other areas. That's fine. I don't expect a church planter to be perfect in each of these categories before planting a church. I would expect them to be confident in their calling, to have the necessary character for ministry leadership, and to be able to

---

[1] For example, Tim Keller identified eighteen characteristics of a church planter. See Timothy J. Keller and J. Allen Thompson, Church Planter Manual (New York: Redeemer City to City, 2002) 69–70.

handle the Word faithfully. Additionally, I would expect them to have confirmation from their local church's leadership (since churches send out church planters). However, since ministry leadership is a journey of a lifetime, these essentials are somewhat aspirational. They are designed to give planters a path of continued development. For instance, we should always seek to improve in our preaching; we should seek to learn best practices for our times; we should seek to grow in our ability to give sound theological answers to the contemporary issues of the day; and we should seek to learn more about what's going on in our cities and among the nations, and how we may effectively engage the world with the gospel.

Faithful Leaders Planting Healthy, Multiplying Communities

The aim of this book is not merely to provide another collection on a bookshelf; rather, the goal is to inspire and instruct in such a way that a greater number of healthier leaders are equipped to plant healthier churches. We need millions of effective church planters and church-planting teams to be deployed across the globe, scattering gospel communities everywhere.

By planting churches, we have the privilege of being in on God's sovereign work in the world. God's redemptive plan has always involved having a people for himself (Titus 2:14; 1 Pet. 2:9–10). When you plant a church, you're not merely starting an event at a storefront, a school, under a tree, in a house, or some other location. Instead, you're participating in God's grand narrative (Acts 18:10)—a story that culminates in John's glorious vision in Revelation where people from every tribe and language and people and nation are giving praise to the Lamb (Rev. 5:1–14). This vision compels us to be faithful in our present generation until the mission is finished.

We get to carry on the Great Commission that Jesus gave us—a task that itself points to church planting. As we go about making disciples among the nations, we are told to do this by *baptizing* and *teaching*, which we see happening in the context of the church (Acts 2:41–47). New believers need to be discipled by faithful pastors and leaders, who will also train and send out more leaders to plant healthy, multiplying churches.

Church planting is the air you breathe when you open the New Testament since it is largely written to a collection of church plants. In the book of Acts, we read of the origin of several of them. What a privilege to be part of this work as we continue this vision! What a responsibility we have for planting and leading healthy, multiplying churches. We have been given a great stewardship.

To Church-planting Team Members

Since the nine essentials are used as an outline for church planter assessment and training, the focus of this book is naturally on the lead church planter. However, since church planting occurs alongside other missional Christians, I would encourage the entire team to read and apply these relevant concepts. What's more, lead planters should read this material with the expectation of church planting *with* others. The New Testament gives us a glorious vision of team planting—including frequent mention of Paul's constant companions, and a host of other servants, who support him on his missionary journeys.

Prayer and the Word

To say church planting is hard is a massive understatement. You will encounter spiritual warfare constantly. Satan hates the work of church planting, and he hates the church you desire to plant. He hates *you*. John says that he rages because "he knows that his time is short!" (Rev. 12:12). We should expect trials and battles, but we aren't left without help. We are invited to commune with the Almighty.

I realize you need more than a book to plant a church. You need the power of God. In light of this, prayer is woven throughout these chapters. You might call it the "essential among the essentials." There are also prayer prompts at the end of each chapter. We need prayer-saturated church planters who lead praying churches.

This book also contains numerous scriptural references. My aim is not to be novel, but clear and biblical about these essentials. Since space limitations prevent me from making longer comments, I recommend looking closely at the cited references and digging deeper into these texts—especially if you can study alongside other leaders. I hope you will find the material warm, engaging, challenging, and hopeful, with plenty of opportunities for practical application along the way.

I love church planters. I love the church. I hope to convey that to you, but remember that Jesus loves you and the church infinitely more than anyone ever could. This good news allows us to rest in him and enjoy him, while we serve him. Our ultimate identity is not in our success as church planters but is found in Christ. We are his, and he is ours, so let us serve the One who loved us and gave himself for us (Gal. 2:20) out of the overflow of a Christ-adoring heart.

"Now to him who is able to do far more abundantly than all that we ask or think, according to the power at work within us, to him be glory in the church and in Christ Jesus throughout all generations, forever and ever. Amen" (Eph. 3:20–21).

1

The Heart

George Mueller was a long-time pastor in England in the nineteenth century who is remembered today mainly for his sacrificial care for orphans (he reportedly cared for over 10,000 orphans in his lifetime). He also did follow-up work for the evangelist D. L. Moody, preached for Charles Spurgeon, inspired the missionary faith of Hudson Taylor, and started a number of other disciple-making ministries.[1] But the secret to Mueller's life is found in his prayer and devotional life. Everything flowed from his consistent walk with God. This spiritual giant once said something I haven't been able to get out of my mind since I first heard it:

> I saw more clearly than ever, that the first great and primary business to which I ought to attend every day, was, to have my soul happy in the Lord.[2]

George was an active, busy man. But he recognized the primary business of the day was to get his heart happy in the Lord. This passion to maintain a vibrant devotional life continued

---

[1] John Piper, "George Mueller's Strategy for Showing God," *Desiring God*, Original Publication February 3, 2004, https://www.desiringgod.org /messages/george-muellers-strategy-for-showing-god.
[2] Ibid.

through the years. At the age of seventy-one, he offered this advice to younger believers:

> Now in brotherly love and affection I would give a few hints to my younger fellow-believers as to the way in which to keep up spiritual enjoyment. It is absolutely needful in order that happiness in the Lord may continue, that the Scriptures be regularly read. These are God's appointed means for the nourishment of the inner man. . . . Consider it, and ponder over it. . . . Especially we should read regularly through the Scriptures, consecutively, and not pick out here and there a chapter. If we do, we remain spiritual dwarfs. I tell you so affectionately. For the first four years after my conversion I made no progress, because I neglected the Bible. But when I regularly read on through the whole with reference to my own heart and soul, I directly made progress. Then my peace and joy continued more and more. Now I have been doing this for 47 years. I have read through the whole Bible about 100 times and I always find it fresh when I begin again. Thus my peace and joy have increased more and more.[3]

We too must seek to prioritize unhurried and unhindered time with God daily, developing a rich and vibrant devotional life that includes the Word and prayer. The trials and temptations of life and ministry are so challenging that we need to get our hearts happy in God by applying the gospel to our lives and communing with our Father in prayer. As we say at Send Network, "Without prayer and the Word, we are powerless." Our communion with the Lord enables us to lead God's people to seek him fervently and frequently for the needs of the church and the advancement of the kingdom.

---

[3] Ibid.

The Heart: Everything You Do Flows from It

The *heart* is the control center for all of life. It is used as a metaphor in Scripture for that which drives all that we do. It reveals what we trust the most, what we love, hope in, and treasure, and what captures our imagination. What we cherish in our hearts controls our lives.[4] A key verse in the Bible's wisdom literature is Proverbs 4:23: "Above all else, guard your heart, for everything you do flows from it" (NIV). We live out of the overflow of our hearts. The Christian life, then, should be lived out of the overflow of a Christ-adoring heart.

The heart affects how we walk and talk. Jesus said, "For out of the abundance of the heart the mouth speaks" (Matt. 12:34). He warns us that sin starts in the heart before it manifests itself in one's behavior: "For from within, out of the heart of man, come evil thoughts, sexual immorality, theft, murder, adultery, coveting, wickedness, deceit, sensuality, envy, slander, pride, foolishness. All these evil things come from within, and they defile a person" (Mark 7:21–23). In the Sermon on the Mount, Jesus said that sexual sin doesn't start externally but internally (Matt. 5:27–30).

The good news of the gospel is that by God's grace, we have received a new heart. We have new life and new capacities (2 Cor. 5:17). We see the world differently and have new power, through the Holy Spirit, to live a life of holiness. But we must continue to guard our hearts and seek to daily fill our affections with the beauty of Jesus. By truly seeking first the kingdom of God (Matt. 6:33), we are empowered to live a life of holiness and humility. Then, we can rest when the day's work is done, entrusting everything to God who rules the world with fatherly sovereignty.

---

[4] Tim Keller, "The Revolutionary Christian Heart," *TimothyKeller.com*, Original Publication February 6, 2015, https://timothykeller.com/blog/2015/2/6/the-revolutionary-christian-heart.

Prayer and the Church Planter

During a class discussion one day related to our reading of E.M. Bounds, we were talking about how men of old got up at 4:00 a.m. to pray. I asked my professor, Dr. Shaddix, "Didn't these guys get up early because they didn't have electricity? I mean, I could get up at 4:00 a.m. if I went to bed at 8:00 p.m." Someone then asked Dr. Shaddix what time he arose to pray. He modestly responded, "Guys, I've been getting up at 4:30 a.m. for the past twelve years in order to spend two hours of unhindered and unhurried time with God. . . . I don't like getting up early, but I realized after I had kids that if I was going to pray without being rushed and distracted, then I needed to get up before they did." I began to slump down in my chair since I woke up at 7:54 on that day to make the 8:00 class! I don't share this story to imply that you need to get up at 4:30 but to reinforce the need to prioritize time with God. (I have found that mornings are best for me.)

Church planters are busy, and it's easy to get straight to work instead of believing that *prayer is the work!* It's easy to be overwhelmed by the anxieties of the day, which is why we need the peace of God that is experienced through faith-filled praying (Phil. 4:6–7). I love what Paul Miller says in A *Praying Life:* "Learning to pray doesn't offer us a less busy life; it offers us a less busy heart."[5]

Further, we must prioritize prayer because only God can bring growth to our ministries (1 Cor. 3:7). Only God can bring sight to the spiritually blind (2 Cor. 4–6; 1 Cor. 2:6–16). When we realize how much we need God to move, how could we not prioritize prayer? Church planters are like farmers. What do farmers do? They get up early, sow, plow, toil, protect, and *beg God for rain.* That's a good description of ministry. Ministry is not glamorous work. Like farming, most of our work is unseen.

---

[5] Paul Miller, A *Praying Life* (Colorado Springs: NavPress, 2009), 25.

It requires constant endurance. It demands constant attention. Still, our work is not enough—we are desperate for God to send the rain so that we may bear fruit.

When pastor Tim Keller decided to leave a respected seminary to go and plant a church in New York City, he described the experience this way:

> [I] felt totally inadequate for the job [planting Redeemer Presbyterian Church]. I know that everyone feels inadequate for any ministry, but this was different. I knew that I was as humanly well-equipped as anyone to try this ministry, but I also knew this was well beyond the human abilities of anyone at all. That meant only one thing for me: it would not be my talent, but my love for, and dependence on, God that would be the critical factor in the project. I felt that my spirituality would be laid bare for all (worst of all, for me) to see.... I prayed and was reading Gurnall's *A Christian in Complete Armour* one day and came upon a passage: "It requires more prowess and greatness of spirit to obey God faithfully than to command an army of men; more greatness to be a Christian than a captain." I realized that it was an illusion to imagine that I would have to start being brave if I took this job [planting Redeemer]; I should have been living bravely all along. Even if I turned the NYC church down, I could not go back to being a coward. So I might as well go to New York! On July 1, I gave Westminster Seminary a year's notice. Immediately, my prayer life broke open like never before.[6]

Church planting should cause your prayer life to break open if you consider how hard it is and what kind of warfare is involved. We go with faith in and reliance on God.

---

[6] Timothy J. Keller and J. Allen Thompson, *Church Planter Manual* (New York: Redeemer, 2002), 10.

Every church planter and church-planting team member who is assessing things properly should be able to resonate with Jehoshaphat's prayer: "For we are powerless against this great horde that is coming against us. We do not know what to do, but our eyes are on you" (2 Chron. 20:12). Amid warfare, the king led the people to seek God desperately. This is godly leadership. It was through this prayerful admission of weakness that God acted in power, winning the battle (2 Chron. 20:13–23). Our strength is not in our giftedness, our age, our biblical knowledge, or our ministry experience. Our strength, this very moment, comes from our union with Christ and is super-charged by our communion with Christ. We live out of our weakness and in the Lord's strength (Heb. 11:32–34).

Pursuing Holiness

Christ-like character flows from a rich communion with God. There needs to be a satisfying delight in God to empower a holy lifestyle. And we shouldn't underestimate the importance of personal holiness in life and ministry. Pastor Robert Murray M'Cheyne said, "The greatest need of my people is my personal holiness."[7]

It's very easy for individuals to rise to leadership in the church because of their gifts and charisma. But if a ministry leader's gifting surpasses his maturity, then he is a walking disaster zone. Unfortunately, stories of moral failure abound because of this very issue: a failure to grow in Christlikeness.

Ongoing growth in holiness is an absolute necessity for ministry leaders for at least three reasons:

---

[7] Kevin DeYoung, "The Pastor's Personal Holiness," *The Gospel Coalition*, Original Publication July 23, 2015, https://www.thegospelcoalition.org/blogs/kevin-deyoung/the-pastors-personal-holiness-2/.

1. Godliness pleases God.
2. The qualifications for pastoral ministry revolve primarily around character, not gifting (with the exception of being able to teach).
3. Godliness makes up for a lot of our deficiencies in ministry.

Personal holiness first requires us to embrace and rejoice in our new identity in Christ. From this heart posture, we are to put off all that is inconsistent with our new life in Christ while putting on all that is consistent with our new life (Col. 3:1–17). Church planters and ministry leaders are to model growth in maturity and lead others to grow in godliness. Not every leader has the same gifting, but all have this calling to grow in Christlikeness and spur God's people on to do the same.

In his classic *Lectures to My Students*, Charles Spurgeon quipped:

> We have all heard the story of the man who preached so well and lived so badly, that when he was in the pulpit everybody said he ought never to come out again, and when he was out of it they all declared he never ought to enter it again... Our character must be more persuasive than our speech.[8]

Sadly, we know of too many stories of ministers whose character was not more persuasive than their words.

Vance Pitman said recently to a group of church planters, "I am one hotel hallway away from destroying my life." Indeed. Whenever you hear of such pastoral failures, remind yourself to take heed lest you too fall (1 Cor. 10:12). John Calvin once said that the human heart is an idol factory. We must seek to put

---

[8] Charles Spurgeon, *Lectures to My Students* (Carol Stream: Tyndale House, 2010), 17.

idols to death and fan our affections for Jesus so that we can walk worthy of the Lord's calling on our lives.

In 1 Timothy 4:11–16, Paul urges Timothy to watch his life and doctrine closely: "Let no one despise you for your youth," he tells him in verse twelve, "but set the believers an example in speech, in conduct, in love, in faith, in purity." So, if others look down upon your youth, don't be tempted to respond with boastful, crass, or hostile behavior. Instead, follow after Christ who is the embodiment of exemplary speech, conduct, love, faith, and purity. If people admire your character, they are less likely to make your age a big deal. By God's grace, let us be above reproach in all things as we live out of the overflow of a heart enthralled by Christ.

Pursuing Humility

The church flourishes under happy, holy, and humble leaders, and it is always moving to hear their testimonies. One of my pastoral heroes, John R. W. Stott, embodied the humble life of a godly shepherd that we read of in the New Testament (see 1 Pet. 5:1–5).

A reporter once asked Stott, "You've had a brilliant academic career; first at Cambridge; Rector at twenty-nine, Chaplain to the Queen; what is your ambition now?" Stott replied, "To be more like Jesus."[9] This was more than a pious answer. Many have given testimony to Stott's humble way of life, drawing attention not only to his prayer life but also his life of servant leadership. The late Ecuadorian theologian and missiologist, René Padilla, told a story of traveling with Stott to Argentina. They arrived late at night in the pouring rain and ended up being quite muddy when arriving at their destination. The following morning Padilla awoke to Stott cleaning Padilla's shoes! When he objected, Stott said, "My

---

[9] Tim Chester, *Stott on the Christian Life* (Wheaton: Crossway, 2020), 225.

dear René, Jesus told us to wash one another's feet. Today we do not wash feet the way people did in Jesus's day, but I can clean your shoes."[10] Stott's long-time secretary, Francis Whitehead, said, "It still amazes me that he emptied my office wastepaper basket every day for many, many years."[11] Ken Perez, who knew Stott well through the London Institute of Contemporary Christianity, said of Stott, "Some people are impressive in public, but disappointing in private. John is the opposite. He is even more impressive in private than in public. His Christ-likeness, gentleness, personal kindness, and authenticity are unforgettable."[12]

This kind of outward behavior is the result of one's interior spiritual life. It shouldn't be a surprise that the same pastor who wrote the classic *The Cross of Christ* had his personal life marked by humility. The more deeply I'm impacted by the work of Jesus on my behalf, the more it will spill over into my actions. A Christ-adoring heart leads to Christlike actions. A life of selfless humility flows from one who has been enamored by Christ (Phil. 2:5–11; John 13:1–17).

Leadership is not lordship. It involves setting a Christ-like example and inviting others to follow you. Jesus has shown us the way. He revolutionized the world with his model of servant leadership. And he has given us power through his saving work on our behalf to follow him in this pursuit of humble servant leadership.

Learning to Rest

They don't write biographies about lazy people. At least, I've never read one! Every great Christian leader I've read about has

---

[10] Ibid.

[11] Ibid.

[12] Ibid.

had a tremendous work ethic. Church planters, therefore, must also be diligent in their work.

I could say a lot about work, but I would like to underscore the importance of rest. It is imperative that church planters find a good rhythm of work and rest, of ministry and recreation, of deep work and peaceful sabbathing. It is easy to idolize work and find your identity in your work. It's easy to burn the candle at both ends and have your mood totally affected by your work. Remember, you are not a machine but an image bearer of God—the God who himself rested (Gen. 2:1–3).

If you do not tend to your heart, you will find it very difficult to rest. My failure to rest is ultimately tied to my failure to trust God (see Ps. 127). I encourage you to find a good rhythm of hard work and quality rest. When working, work. When resting, rest. Learn to find things that are life-giving on your day off.

In his book *Reset*, David Murray talks about retired Pastor Al Martin's counsel to young ministers who were just months into their ministries. They would say things like, "Please help me. I can't pray. I can't study. I can't sleep. I can't go on. I think I'm going to resign." To this kind of statement, Martin responded: "Here's your problem. You're trying to live like a disembodied angel rather than flesh-and-blood humanity. Here's your solution: first, exercise vigorously at least three times per week. Second, take a full day off a week. And third, spend at least one evening a week with your wife alone." When the young ministers would push back, complaining about his plan, he would conclude, "Do these three things and call me back next month."[13] He said he's never been called back! We're not disembodied angels. We are image bearers of God who need rest.

---

[13] David Murray, *Reset: Living a Grace-Paced Life in a Burnout Culture* (Wheaton: Crossway, 2017), 40.

As you practice these rhythms, remember that Jesus offers the kind of rest that a vacation can't give you. We are not saved by our ministry performance but through the finished work of Jesus. Rest in his grace daily and set aside particular days to completely cease your labor and focus on your family, the enjoyment of creation, life-giving activities, and physical respite.

Living in Community

One of the gifts God has given us to pursue a life marked by happiness in Jesus, holiness of character, and humility before God and others is *the community of faith*. Even if you are a Christian leader, do not neglect the need to share your life with other believers. Isolation is dangerous. We need other believers to spur us on to love and good deeds. We need accountability. We need encouragement.

A life of holiness and humility is a community project. So, let us participate in the functions of the church like a "normal" Christian. We need to be part of the weekly worship gathering, and we also benefit from other brothers and sisters exhorting us in community (Heb. 10:19–25).

In the case of Christian leaders who've had a terrible fall, it usually starts with the neglect of their time with God and their lack of participation in Christian community. Be wise, church planter. Tend to your heart and stay in community.

In his book *Dangerous Calling*, Paul Tripp describes many of the problems within a spiritually unhealthy pastoral culture. One of the points he zeros in on is missing community. After sharing his experience with the problematic "Me and Jesus" version of Christianity, he says, "I have now come to understand that I need others in my life. I now know that I need to commit myself to living in an intentionally intrusive, Christ-centered, grace-driven, redemptive community. I now know that it's my job to seek this community out, to invite people to interrupt my private conversation, and to say things to me that I couldn't or wouldn't say to myself."[14] In his grace, God has given us the community of faith. Don't neglect it, church leader, but press into it.

Conclusion

It is vital that we guard our hearts. The heart controls our actions, and everything we do flows from it. Therefore, let us daily practice the means of grace God has given us, including prayer, Bible reading, and Christian community, so we can live lives of holiness and humility from a Christ-adoring heart as we pour out our lives for the kingdom.

---

[14] Paul David Tripp, *Dangerous Calling* (Wheaton: Crossway, 2012), 84.

Prayer Prompts

- Holy Father, teach us to guard our hearts, knowing that everything we do flows from them.
- Help us to be holy and humble, and give us Christ-adoring hearts from which we pour out our lives for your kingdom.
- Make us men and women who work hard, rest well, and live in Christian community.
- May we seek first your kingdom in all we say and do, as you align our hearts with yours.

Reflection Questions

1. What spiritual "vital signs" could you point to that would demonstrate your communion with Christ?
2. How are you seeing God answer your prayers?
3. What areas of your life have you seen God grow you in maturity? Where are you still weak?
4. How have you observed a life of godliness making up for deficiencies in your ministry giftedness?

Relationships

Before my first semester of seminary, I was so eager to begin my studies that I devoured the seminary catalog. However, as I surveyed the programs and required courses for my degree, one class puzzled me: Interpersonal Relationship Skills. Why would a future pastor or ministry leader need this course? I mean, biblical studies and theology made sense, but this class seemed unnecessary. I remember someone later telling me that the development of the course was the result of research on why graduates had a hard time in the local church. Their problems weren't due to their theology or preaching skills, but their failure to cultivate and maintain healthy relationships. Matters like handling conflict, collaborating with others, dealing with difficult people, and showing hospitality are not matters of marginal importance. It's vital for a Christian leader to be good with people.

Having been in pastoral ministry for some twenty years, I have observed many leaders who were great with theology but terrible with people. That simply won't work in ministry. Ministry work is people work. Of course, the opposite is true also— some are good with people and terrible at theology. We need to be good at both!

We must lead people humbly (1 Pet. 5:1–5), love people genuinely (1 Tim. 4:12; 2 Tim. 4:22), deal with conflict peaceably (Matt. 5:9; Rom. 14:19), deal with critics gently (2 Tim. 2:25), and love outsiders warmly (1 Tim. 3:7; Titus 1:8). We have the joy of collaborating with other gospel-driven people on mission as well. Further, Paul says overseers (if they are married) must love their wives faithfully (1 Tim. 3:2) and manage their households well (1 Tim. 3:4–5; Titus 1:6). Relationships matter—in the home, in the church, in a church-planting network, and in the outside world.

Honoring Christ in our relationships by following the teaching of Scripture is the calling given to all Christians—whether or not one is in vocational ministry. The unique challenge for church planters and ministry leaders is to set the believers *an example* in this area (1 Tim. 4:12).

Healthy Relationships

One could look to several texts to think about healthy relationships, but a go-to passage for me is Romans 12:9–21.

Romans 12 marks a new section in Paul's letter to the Romans. Believers are exhorted to live in view of God's mercies—the glorious gospel that we read about in Romans 1–11. We are to offer our bodies as "a living sacrifice" to God (12:1) and be transformed through the renewal of our minds (12:2). Christians can primarily live out Romans 12:1–2 by giving themselves to the church through the use of their spiritual gifts (12:3–8) and performing gospel-centered acts of love in their relationships (12:9–16).

In Romans, we find Paul dealing with a conflict between Jews and gentiles (see 14:1) with the church having fractured along ethnic lines. Since the leadership was mainly gentile, meetings were being held in house churches instead of synagogues, and the Jewish believers would have found many of the gentile cultural practices offensive. All of this gives rise to Paul's glorious multi-ethnic vision for the people of God.

Romans 12:9–21 is not that difficult to understand, but it's difficult to *live*! That's because it's about relationships. I'm reminded of the *Charlie Brown* cartoon where Lucy tells Linus that he could never become a doctor because he doesn't love mankind. Linus quips, "I love mankind; it's people I can't stand." It's easy to love the *idea* of the church, but quite another thing to love real people in the church. This is why we need the regular renewal of our minds. Renewed minds lead to new attitudes, relationships, and practices that are not conformed to this world.

The fact is, if these verses were lived out faithfully, our world would be radically changed. The counter-cultural church certainly changed the first-century Greco-Roman world, which existed as *a little outpost of the kingdom of God*. They lived out these instructions in a hierarchical culture marked by honor and shame. In doing so, they said to the world, "If you want to know what the kingdom is like—here's a glimpse. It's not perfect, but it's a glimpse." In God's kingdom, there's love and honor, passion and perseverance, generosity and hospitality, rejoicing and weeping, harmony and humility, and goodness and peacemaking.

Paul essentially urges the Romans to allow *the gospel* to shape and empower their relationships with others in six distinct ways:

1. Love and Honor (12:9–10)

Paul says, "Let love be genuine" (12:9a), serving as a kind of header over the whole section. Real love is sincere. Christian love is never to be a guise for ulterior motives. As planters and ministry leaders, we're called to genuinely love the people in our care, and not see them as "numbers" or as a means to some end.

Paul helps us avoid a misunderstanding of love when he says, "Abhor what is evil; hold fast to what is good" (12:9b). Love doesn't allow evil to persist in the name of "love." Love *hates* certain things. We are to pursue holy love. Love is not genuine when it leads a person to do something evil, allows a person to do evil, or avoids addressing evil. Love knows the difference between right and wrong (1 Cor. 13:6). Good parents don't allow their kids to do just anything in the name of love, and good pastors will also address evil as an act of love for the church fellowship.

Further, this genuine love is marked by "brotherly affection" (12:10a). Christians should seek to cultivate tenderness, warmth, and affection. In his *Lectures to My Students*, pastor Charles Spurgeon exhorted his students to cultivate this kind of heart, saying:

> I love a minister whose face invites me to make him my friend. . . on whose doorstep you read "Welcome," not "Beware of Dog." . . . Give me the man around whom the children come. . . . An individual who doesn't have a friendly, cheerful manner about him had better be an undertaker, and bury the dead, for he will never succeed in influencing the living. . . . A man must have a great heart if he is to have a great congregation. . . . When a man has a large, loving heart, men go to him as ships to a haven. . . . Such a man is hearty in private as well as in public.[1]

May God make us these kinds of leaders!

Regarding *honor*, Paul says to the church, "Outdo one another in showing honor" (12:10b). This was a radical command in the hierarchical, first-century world (Rom. 12:17; 13:7; 1 Pet. 2:17).

---

[1] Spurgeon, *Lectures to My Students* (Carol Stream: Tyndale House, 2010), 168–69.

I'm always struck by the kind of respect Paul conveyed as he preached the gospel to Felix and Agrippa at the end of Acts. It is also striking how Paul honored faithful servants in the church throughout his letters (Rom. 16:1–16). As planters and ministry leaders, look for ways to honor faithful servants in the church.

2. Passion and Perseverance (12:11–12)

The next verse drips with passion: "Do not be slothful in zeal, be fervent in spirit, serve the Lord" (12:11). Christian love is not cold or indifferent! In the previous passage, Paul said that those with the gift of leadership must lead "with zeal" (12:8). That is, we are to be set on fire by the Spirit who empowers our leadership (12:11), and we should keep in constant view the focus of our ministry: serving the Lord. Jesus is the object of our zeal. Demonstrating a passion for Christ and compassion for his people is at the heart of faithful ministry.

Romans 12 hangs over my bed in my home: "Rejoice in hope, be patient in tribulation, be constant in prayer." The theme of perseverance ties these three phrases together. Life and ministry are hard, but we can derive hope and joy in Christ, and we can find strength through prayer. How do we endure "tribulation" without murmuring and self-pity? By *rejoicing* and *praying*. If a ministry leader is not rejoicing and praying, then that leader won't be persevering.

3. Generosity and Hospitality (12:13)

Two practical ways to love and pursue harmony are generosity and hospitality. Christian leaders are to set an example of generosity (Acts 4:36–37; 20:35) and must never be driven by greed (1 Tim. 6:5; 1 Pet. 5:2). Rather, we are to be cheerful givers, as we remember that our God is a giver, too (Rom. 8:32).

Further, we are to welcome others as we have been welcomed by God in Christ (Rom. 15:7; Isa. 25:6–7; 55:1–3; Matt.

11:28; Luke 14:12–24; Rev. 21:3). Peter urges Christians to do this without grumbling (1 Pet. 4:9). Here in Romans 12, Paul speaks of the intentionality of hospitality, exhorting us to *pursue* it.

For pastors, hospitality is a qualification for ministry (1 Tim. 3:2). If one does not welcome others into their home, their church, and their lives, then that person doesn't belong in ministry. This practice is vital for pastoral ministry, for evangelism and mercy ministry, and for the work of church planting.

4. Rejoicing and Weeping (12:15)

In Romans 15, Paul says: "Rejoice with those who rejoice, weep with those who weep." All Christians are to come alongside their brothers and sisters in the highs and lows of life, with pastors setting the believers an example in this area. When one person succeeds, rejoice with them! And when they are hurting, weep with them.

Many Christian leaders have a ministry of *truth* but not a ministry of *tears*. Jesus displayed both. He brought people the words of life and he wept at Lazarus's tomb—even though he knew he was about to raise him to life. The Good Shepherd in John 10 demonstrated his pastoral care in John 11. He entered into the grief of his friends and wept with them (John 11:35). We, too, need an integrated ministry of both mind and heart, emotions and theology, tears and truth.

5. Harmony and Humility (12:16)

Paul tells the Roman Christians, "Live in harmony with one another" (12:16a). He later prays for such harmony (15:5). This unity reflected the nature of God and offered a powerful witness to the world. An ongoing challenge in ministry is helping brothers and sisters deal with conflict, hurt feelings, and misunderstanding. Harmony takes hard work. The kind of harmony we're after is not merely an absence of strife but the presence of unity (Ps. 133).

To have harmony, *humility* must be present: "Do not be haughty, but associate with the lowly. Never be wise in your own sight" (Rom. 12:16b). This principle is taught elsewhere in the New Testament (Phil. 2:1–4). One of the signs of humility is associating with all kinds of people. As church leaders, we should constantly evaluate our own lives to ensure that we are pursuing humility, but we must also teach and lead in such a way that we're fostering humility in the church.

6. Goodness and Peacemaking (12:14, 17–21)

In Romans 12:14, Paul reflects on the teaching of Jesus regarding our enemies (Matt. 5:44; Luke 6:28). Notice we're not simply to refrain from retaliating, nor should we simply forgive our enemies. Instead, we're to actively seek their good as we pray for God's blessing on them! This verse is particularly relevant for those in ministry because there are many adversaries out there.

In Romans 17–21, Paul highlights more action steps regarding our relationships with our enemies, emphasizing non-retaliation and peacemaking. We're to seek to live honorably among everyone, to do everything we can to live peaceably with all, and to leave vengeance to God. He ends the section with a summary admonition: "Do not be overcome by evil, but overcome evil with good" (12:21). We must disciple and counsel our members in this area.

Of course, on a civil level, we need courts and law enforcement. Paul isn't teaching that we should allow abuse or violence to go unchecked. The very next passage (Rom. 13:1–7) emphasizes that the state has the right to bear the sword, and that God has appointed the government as the institution to carry out judgment on Earth. As good citizens, we need to promote biblical justice now, but ultimately trust in the Lord's final judgment in the future.

A Healthy Marriage

You obviously don't have to be married to be a church planter or be on a church-planting team. After all, the greatest church planter ever, the apostle Paul, wasn't married! And I could list many other faithful planters/pastors who were or currently are single. In fact, there are some great advantages to not being married, as Paul describes in 1 Corinthians 7. However, many church planters are married, and this subject is significant for several reasons.

Over the past few years, I've learned of some well-known church leaders who were removed from ministry due to unfaithfulness in marriage. Interestingly, the men I have in mind were known for having regular morning devotional times. However, their marriages weren't healthy, and each of these men was unfaithful to his wife. I have since grown to see how one can envision personal holiness in a privatized way while neglecting relational holiness. Married men: The pursuit of your wife and the cultivation of a faithful and joyful marriage *must* be at the heart of your pursuit of holiness. If not, then you are a walking disaster zone.

The Foundation for Marriage

The first place we turn to on this subject is the opening chapters of Genesis. Marriage is God's idea (Matt. 19:4–6).

In the beginning, God created everything. He is God over it all. But one thing isn't good: a man alone. So, God decides to make a suitable "helper" for Adam (Gen. 2:18). Genesis 1:27 tells us that God created "man in his own image," equal in value and dignity, as "male and female." The creation of Eve led to the first union between man and woman—a holy, one-flesh union and a complementary relationship (Eph. 5:22–33).

Marriage is for partnership. At the foundation of a healthy marriage is companionship (Prov. 2:17). The author of Song of Solomon declared, "This is my beloved and this is my friend" (5:16b). Initially, Adam had animals, but he didn't have a wife! One of the great gifts in marriage is *companionship*. If you are in a covenant marriage, let me encourage you to have fun together!

My wife and I met while working at a Christian youth camp (a stereotypical story, I know!) and were married a few years later. We have only known each other in the context of doing ministry together, and this has been a tremendous blessing. She truly is my dear companion and my partner in ministry. Show me a faithful church planter who is bearing much fruit, and more times than not, you will hear him testify to how his bride is laboring side by side with him. She may not be doing the same things other pastors' wives are doing, but she's there as his companion in life and ministry.

Marriage is for procreation. Procreation is not the only purpose of marriage, and a church planter doesn't need to have children. However, one of the divine purposes of marriage is to "be fruitful and multiply" (Gen. 1:28). The church views children as wonderful gifts from God (Ps. 127–128). One of the blessings of community is investing in and caring for one another's children.

Marriage is for pleasure. While many may blush at the idea of talking about the goodness of sex within marriage, it shouldn't be ignored (1 Cor. 7:1–5). To be sure, there are other pleasures in marriage, but this has to be at the top of the list (Heb. 13:4). The writer of Proverbs teaches men to find their pleasure in the wife of their youth (Prov. 5:18–20). Further, the writer of Song of Solomon speaks in vivid terms about enjoying each other.

If you are married and in ministry, it is important to cultivate romance in your marriage. A good marriage is not only one that you *endure* but one that you *enjoy*. Marriages that contain frequent intimate experiences offer several advantages, like keeping the tempter away (1 Cor. 7:5b). Satan would love to keep married couples away from each other.

Marriage is a symbol. Marriage embodies the covenant-keeping love of Christ for his bride—the church (Eph. 5:22–33). This fact should constantly amaze us. After citing Genesis 2:24, Paul writes, "This mystery is profound, and I am saying that it refers to Christ and the church" (Eph. 5:32). Nowhere else in the world do people have such a view of marriage as those who embrace this biblical vision.

The point of marriage is ultimately not the relationship between husband and wife but between Christ and his church. Borrowing a line I heard, I've often quipped, "Kimberly and I have a perfect marriage. It's just not with each other! It's with Christ." While we do have a wonderful marriage, for which I give God praise, our marriage is not ultimately about us. Yours isn't ultimately about you and your spouse. Since we are united with Christ, and because of the temporary nature of marriage, there's freedom in knowing we don't have to idolize marriage. Even if you have a great marriage, it's a shadow of the glorious union to come. And if some things aren't right in your marriage, it's okay to admit that right now and begin to seek help, change, and grow.

The Bible begins and ends with a wedding (Gen. 2:18; Rev. 19:6). If that weren't significant enough, Jesus's first miracle was at a wedding. In Scripture, first things are important things. When Jesus turns water into wine at a wedding (John 2:1–11),

John calls this miracle a "sign" (2:11), pointing to the greater story that's being told. Not only has Jesus come to give joy, but his first miracle is a foretaste of a greater wedding, a greater feast, a greater party to come.

Whether you are a single minister or a married one, let us all stand in awe of this reality. This is where we want to lead everyone to: Jesus Christ, the Lord of the Feast, the Groom of the Bride. Jesus provides the greatest of all unions and the best of joys.

May the Lord give those of you who are married a marathon marriage. May your marriage bring you great joy, may it bring God glory, and may it point others to the ultimate union of Christ and his bride.

Conclusion

Relationships matter in Christian life, and church planters and ministry leaders should set the believers an example in cultivating and maintaining Christ-honoring relationships. The gospel must be proclaimed by church leaders, but the gospel must also shape and empower our relationships with those inside and outside the church. Additionally, married church planters should seek to cultivate a godly marriage with their spouses.

Prayer Prompts

- Holy Father, as husbands and fathers, help us to love and lead our families in ways that point others to you.
- Help us to cultivate healthy relationships and lead our churches to do likewise.
- Give us the grace to treat others honorably, setting an example for others to follow.
- Bless our relationships, giving us unity and helping us to resolve any conflicts in ways that honor Christ.

Reflection Questions

1. How are you seeking to cultivate and maintain healthy relationships? Who are some of the people with whom you have cultivated close relationships? How long have you known them, and what do your conversations sound like?
2. How has your practice of hospitality built community around you?
3. How do you think your wife would describe your care and spiritual leadership toward her and your family (as it relates to time, money, parenting, affection, intimacy, and so on)?
4. What are your three greatest strengths and weaknesses as a husband and a father?

Additional Questions for the Wife of a Prospective Church Planter

1. Do you believe your husband possesses the spiritual, moral, and emotional maturity necessary to serve as a pastor-planter? Are there any issues in your husband's life, your life, or your family's life that might make it

wise for your husband *not* to be a pastor-planter at this time?

2. How convinced are you that God is leading your family to be part of planting a church?

3. What sacrifices are you willing to make to see this come to fruition? What sacrifices are you unwilling to make?

4. In what ways do you personally hope to contribute to this missional endeavor? What aspects or potential expectations might you want to avoid?

3

Calling

My friend Adam Muhtaseb, whom our church had the pleasure of sending out to plant a church in Baltimore, explained his conversion by saying, "When Islam choked me with 'Do, do, do,' Jesus said, 'It's already done,' and captured my heart. That's how a Muslim kid eventually became a Christian church planter in one of America's most unreached cities."[1]

Between his glorious conversion and his planting of Redemption City Church in Baltimore, I had the privilege of watching him mature and develop. In addition to having a robust gospel-centered theology, Adam had two things all church planters need: a personal calling to plant a church and a willingness to be patient until his elders confirmed that he was ready.

In fact, Adam had first been urged to plant a church immediately after doing some fruitful college ministry in Maryland. However, he sensed that he needed to learn more, be commended by mature leaders, and be sent out from a healthy local church. So, he came to be with us in North Carolina for a season. I have had a front-row seat watching this process, and now

---

[1] Adam Muhtaseb, "The Secret to Church Planting (From a Former Muslim)," *The Gospel Coalition*, Original Publication July 7, 2020, https://www.thegospelcoalition.org/article/secret-church-planting/.

celebrate the impact he and his church are making in a hard city.

Calling and *commendation* bring together the inward desire to start a church along with outside affirmation from other leaders. Calling speaks to one's inner conviction, ambition, or aspiration for the work. Commendation speaks to the need for others to recognize and affirm the planter's gifts and maturity required for the work. Both serve to provide *confidence* in the life of the church planter.

Calling

Every follower of Jesus is called to be a minister in a general sense. As priests of God (1 Pet. 2:4–10), every Christian can take God to people (in witness), and people to God (in prayer). Basic gospel ministry is not reserved exclusively for those in vocational ministry.

In Ephesians, Paul urges all believers to "walk in a manner worthy of the calling to which you have been called" (4:1). He also describes some essential characteristics of the believer's lifestyle (4:2–3), the basis for Christian unity (4:4–6), and how God has gifted his church for service (4:7–10). But then he identifies those who are called and gifted in *a unique sense* and are tasked with the role of equipping the saints for works of ministry (Eph. 4:11–12).

How, then, do you know if you have been called to this kind of leadership role in the church? Not everyone agrees on this subject (nor on the nature of the offices listed in Ephesians 4:11). It's not my purpose to engage in these debates, but I do want to argue that there is such a thing as a calling to ministry leadership.

Paul believed he had been *appointed to the ministry* (1 Tim. 1:12). While recognizing the uniqueness of Paul's role in the mission of God, I believe the Lord is still calling people to ministry leadership, including the work of church planting.

This is vital because the work of ministry is too demanding to enter without a sense of calling. It's also a glorious privilege. Regarding the call to preach, D. Martyn Lloyd-Jones said, "To me the work of preaching is the highest and the greatest and the most glorious calling to which anyone can ever be called."[2] Martin Luther said something similar years earlier, "If I could today become king or emperor, I would not give up my office as a preacher."[3]

One's *specific* calling into the ministry may become clearer over time. Some sense a call to be in ministry initially but are unsure of what form that will take. This was my experience. The specific shape and form of our ministry may develop progressively rather than immediately. Our calling may also even change slightly from season to season.

A Holy Ambition

In Romans 15:14–33, the apostle Paul describes his calling, past travels, and future plans for ministry. As he does, he says something significant regarding this idea of conviction, aspiration, or as he calls it, "ambition" (Rom. 15:20). We get a glimpse inside the heart of this great missionary and church planter as he writes:

> I make it my ambition to preach the gospel, not where Christ has already been named, lest I build on someone else's foundation, but as it is written, "Those who have never been told of him will see, and those who have never heard will understand." (Rom. 15:20-21)

---

[2] D. Martyn Lloyd-Jones, *Preaching and Preachers* (Grand Rapids: Zondervan, 2012) 9.

[3] Quoted in Fred W. Meuser, *Luther the Preacher* (Minneapolis: Ausberg, 1983), 39.

The act of preaching Christ where he was neither named nor known consumed the apostle Paul. Like modern-day church planters, his burning conviction to do this work made him willing to make great sacrifices.

John Piper describes Paul's desire as a "holy ambition," and emphasizes that all Christians should have some kind of holy ambition.[4] While not everyone will share Paul's vision for pioneer evangelism and church planting, all Christians should be driven by the Great Commission and God's glory.

Not every aspiring church leader will go into church planting. Some will build on someone else's foundation (1 Cor. 3:5–11) and lead established churches (1 Tim. 3:1). This is a good thing. We certainly need faithful pastors to step into existing local churches and lead faithfully. But some ministers will have a desire like Paul's, eager to start from scratch in underserved and unreached areas. They will long to bring the gospel to hard places and see new churches started. This holy ambition drives their work.

Paul's *passion* inspires us to "fan into flame" the gifts God has given us (2 Tim. 1:6). His example is an important reminder that people who make a tremendous gospel impact in the world are not always the most gifted; they are simply those most devoted to the cause. The secret to faithful church planting is not mastering a set of techniques and methods, but being mastered by theological, spiritual, and missional convictions.

Further, observe that Paul's ambition wasn't a personal agenda, but one driven by *Scripture*. In Romans 15:21, he quotes Isaiah 52:15, expecting that the nations will be greatly amazed by the "Suffering Servant." Paul longed to preach to people who had not been "told" nor had ever "heard" the good news, encouraged by the expectation that many would subsequently

---

[4] John Piper, "A Holy Ambition," a sermon available at https://www.desiringgod.org/messages/holy-ambition.

hear and embrace Jesus. Church planters also go into the world with confidence that God has a people for himself and that as the gospel is proclaimed, many will respond in faith (Acts 18:10).

Scholar Tom Schreiner states that Paul would have been about sixty years old when stating this holy ambition![5] This vision of a sixty-year-old, war-torn apostle desiring to go to Spain to reach unreached people groups and start new churches is truly inspiring. His conviction was born out of Scripture, likely with deep reflection on Isaiah's vision of the coastlands hearing the good news (Isa. 11:11; 41:1; 42:4, 10; 49:1; 51:5; 52:15; 60:9; 66:19–20). Aspiring church planters need to follow Paul's example and be driven by Scripture, meditating on the Word of God day and night to get direction, deepen their theological and missional convictions, and embolden them for the work ahead.

Piper comments:

> When Jesus called Paul on the Damascus road to take the gospel to the Gentiles who had never heard, Paul went to the Old Testament and looked for a confirmation and explanation of this calling to see how it fit into God's overall plan. And he found it. And for our sake he speaks this way. He doesn't just refer to his experience on the Damascus road, which we will never have. He refers to God's written word that we do have. And he roots his ambition there.[6]

Church planters, this holy ambition, this consuming gospel passion, will keep you from fizzling out or giving up. Ministry is not for the faint of heart, and church planting is laborious. If

---

[5] Tom Schreiner, "Proclaiming the Gospel to the Ends of the Earth," a sermon available at https://cliftonbaptist.org/media/sqc5zh5/proclaiming-the-gospel-to-the-ends-of-the-earth.

[6] Ibid.

one ever envisions church planting as glamorous, they only need to read about Paul's afflictions (2 Cor. 6:3–10; 11:23b–28). He traveled hundreds and hundreds of miles—and was not doing so in a nice Hummer with air conditioning! Advancing the gospel always requires sacrifice, and church planting will bring with it a host of challenges. You will face spiritual opposition (2 Cor. 4:3–4). You may even face violent opposition from people. You will be tempted to grow discouraged or anxious. You will have to deal with conflict among your people. There will be long days of doing all sorts of things (meetings, emails, fundraising, sermon prep, counseling, writing, prayer, and more). Nevertheless, we go in the Lord's strength (2 Tim. 2:1; Eph. 6:10), compelled by a holy ambition to make Christ known and to see churches planted.

Heart Questions

Potential church planters need to wrestle with important heart questions like: Do I have an intense, all-absorbing desire for this work? Am I willing to make hard sacrifices for this mission?

Trying to discern whether or not one should plant a new church often becomes clearer over time. When I went to seminary, I knew I wanted to preach and do ministry, but I wasn't exactly sure what this would look like. I loved evangelistic preaching and student ministry, but eventually church planting became a passionate desire.

Interestingly, a class on church administration impacted me. In this class, we studied all kinds of things related to the church. I had never thought much before about childcare check-in, parking lot workers, deacon ministry, hospital visitation, pastoral rhythms, small-group methods, and many other practical matters. Reflecting on Romans 15:20 and these course lectures, I began asking myself: *What would it look like if I started a church that wasn't built on anyone else's foundation?* I didn't immediately plant a church then, but this burning desire never left me. My wife and I discussed church planting regularly until Imago Dei Church was eventually planted in Raleigh in 2011.

You don't go into church planting because you think it's cool, to prove something to others, or to boost your ego. Faithful church planters are driven by spiritual convictions that have been born out of deep thought and prayer, and a strong sense of the Lord's providential guidance.

Commendation

Church planters should never operate as lone rangers. While it is good and right to have an inward compulsion to plant a church, this should be accompanied by the external confirmation of others. Paul told Timothy, "Do not be hasty in the laying on of hands" (1 Tim. 5:22). We should not rush to put one in ministry leadership. This is for the good of the leader but also for the sake of the church they lead. A proper assessment of the candidate and a period of observation is crucial. What should others observe? I'll mention four key characteristics.

1. Maturity

Paul warns about giving spiritual leadership to "a recent convert" (1 Tim. 3:6). Maturity is mandatory for ministry leadership (2 Tim. 2:22–26; 3:10–11). Mature leaders in the congregation have a responsibility to identify and affirm new mature leaders (Titus 1:5–9).

In Acts 16, Paul takes Timothy with him on his missionary journey. Luke tells us that Timothy was "well spoken of by the brothers" (Acts 16:2). Though young, Timothy displayed a sense of maturity, and the saints in Lystra and Iconium approved of him accompanying Paul. We also see confirmation of spiritual affirmation and approval when Paul speaks of the elders laying their hands on Timothy (1 Tim. 4:14).

There are many sad stories of gifted leaders who were put in leadership roles before they were ready to be there. It is often hard to strike a balance between the urgency of the mission and sufficient observation of maturity, but aspiring ministry leaders need to exhibit godliness before being sent out for the work.

2. Desire

Godly people should also see in a potential planter a real desire for kingdom work. They should observe a hunger for Scripture. They should detect humility and an enjoyment of ministry. They should see a passion and a willingness to sacrifice for the mission. Close friends and one's spouse (if married) should be able to attest to these things as well. If married, it's critical that the planter's wife also shares a passion for gospel ministry and church planting.

Speaking about entering the ministry in general, Charles Spurgeon said, "'Do not enter the ministry if you can help it,' was the deeply sage advice of a divine to one who sought his judgment. If any student in this room could be a newspaper editor, or a grocer, or a farmer, or a doctor, or a lawyer, or a senator, or a king, in the name of heaven and earth let him go his way."[7] This does not mean that you can't be both a lawyer and a church planter—you most certainly can!—but it does highlight the importance of having a *desire* for ministry.

Indeed, the call to ministry involves great passion. Paul says, "If anyone *aspires* to the office of overseer, he *desires* a noble

---

[7] Charles Spurgeon, *Lectures to My Students* (Grand Rapids: Zondervan, 1954, reprint), 26–27.

task" (1 Tim. 3:1, emphasis mine). When Paul spoke about preaching, he also displayed this passion: "For if I preach the gospel, that gives me no ground for boasting. For necessity is laid upon me. Woe to me if I do not preach the gospel!" (1 Cor. 9:16). This kind of passion—for gospel ministry in general and church planting in particular—should be something other mature Christians see in aspiring planters.

3. Abilities

Church planters also need to display certain gifts necessary for ministry. They should be able to minister the Word faithfully and effectively (1 Tim. 3:2). They should be good at engaging unbelievers. They should be able to gather a team and lead others spiritually. Godly leaders should see in them the ability to make the most of gospel opportunities with the gifts God has given them.

Tim Keller comments on the importance of one's skills and abilities, and the value of experienced leaders speaking into the potential planter's life:

> The success in starting a new church is largely determined by who is selected as the church planter. To establish a new church requires of the church planter distinct gifts, skills and experiences in ministry often not found in a normal pastor. Though there are many similarities in these two roles, the church planter must thrive in outreach ministry and in developing and empowering new leaders. Although self-evaluation is important in understanding one's gifts and call, much can be learned by inviting the objective evaluation of experienced church planters.[8]

---

[8] Timothy J. Keller and J. Allen Thompson, *Church Planter Manual* (New York: Redeemer, 2002), 68.

Going through a church-planting assessment is one way we take this external confirmation seriously. At our church, the pastors assess our planters, and we ask several people to comment on their maturity and gifts. In Send Network, we also take church-sent candidates through a rigorous assessment process.

While this assessment can be painful because it opens one up to critique, it's also a wonderful blessing as it serves to bring awareness to weaknesses in a biblically supportive context. This can set the planter on a path to growing in specific areas, with the motivation for doing so. Ministry leaders are lifelong learners. We should always be growing.

Further, a good assessment process can prevent many problems in the future. This includes, but is not limited to, burnout, marital issues, theological errors, and financial problems—all of which not only hurt the leader but also the new church. It also assists faithful stewardship as the churches and/or denominations that are supporting the planter need to know that their character and abilities have been properly considered.

Finally, a good assessment can give confidence to the church planter and his wife (if applicable). When a church planter knows that his life and skills have been considered closely and that wise leaders approve of their church-planting work, that sense of settled assurance means a ton.

4. Fruitfulness

Mature leaders should see evidence that others have been blessed by the potential planter's ministry in some particular way. For example, when he has the opportunity to teach or preach, his ministry has a gospel impact. He's able to disciple others into maturity, and he engages lost people well. Perhaps others have observed his ability to lead a small group faithfully.

If a potential planter has not made any disciples or displayed any ministry fruitfulness, then it begs the question: Does he possess the ability to plant a church and lead a group of people on mission?

One of the tasks of planters/pastors is to always be on the lookout for future leaders and planters. In addition to having a "to-do list," one pastor said we should also have a "to-be list." We should always be looking for faithful, budding leaders who display maturity, passion, gifting, and fruitfulness. Identifying them, investing in them, and sending them out on mission is a vitally important aspect of pastoral leadership.

Never Get Over It

We should never get over the wonder of being called to serve King Jesus. My long-time pastor-friend David Platt reminded me of this in a rather unforgettable way. He was in town preaching at a seminary chapel service, and we had a great chat over some tea (one of David's only flaws is that he doesn't like coffee), before heading our separate ways. As I backed out of the driveway, I said, "David, let's stay in touch more often. I miss talking to you." It was one of those "call a brother, will you?" moments. Instead of giving me a courteous response, David replied with, "We should be in hell, bro." *Wow, that escalated quickly!* I wasn't ready for that comeback. After pausing to reflect for a moment, I said, "I know. Can you believe we get to do what we do? It's truly amazing."

His comment left me with a profound sense of awe and gratitude to God who has called us to ministry. David's point was that he and I have no business doing ministry. It's purely by the mercy of God (1 Tim. 1:12–13; 2 Cor. 4:1). I determined to remind myself of this every single day. "I'm not in hell today" puts things in perspective, right? Reminding myself that no condemnation awaits me, I have been cleansed, I'm loved, and I'm in the King's family changes everything. The King of Kings wants me to offer my time, talent, and treasure to him. Gladly! It's a sheer privilege to serve Jesus in his mission.

Conclusion

Church planters are driven by deep, personal convictions, born out of Scripture, deep thought, and a sense of the Lord's guidance. Their passion for planting a new church means they're willing to work hard and make sacrifices. But they also recognize the need for others to commend them for the work and should not be hasty in the process. Mature leaders should see evidence of their holy ambition, spiritual maturity, ability to lead a new church, and fruitfulness in the aspiring planter's present ministry. To start healthier, multiplying churches, church leaders need to invest seriously in aspiring planters, emphasizing both internal calling and external commendation.

Prayer Prompts

- Heavenly Father, raise up generations of men with a holy ambition to engage their cities with the gospel, make disciples of Jesus, and plant churches for your great glory on earth.
- Make us men who seek you, praying with others for affirmation of your calling on our lives.
- Help us to identify and raise up the new leaders you've called to continue in the ministry of church planting.
- Fill us with the maturity, desire, abilities, and fruitfulness we need to plant healthy, multiplying churches in our cities and beyond so more people may know and worship you.

Reflection Questions

1. Consider for a moment the issues of leadership, context, and timing. Why do you think God might be leading you to plant a church? Why you? Why there? Why now?
2. What passages of Scripture has God used to cultivate within you a desire for the work of church planting?
3. What sacrifices are you willing to make to see a church formed? What sacrifices are you unwilling to make?
4. Who can speak to your maturity as a leader, your desire for this work, the gifts God has given you, and your fruitfulness in ministry? How have they affirmed you thus far?

4

Theology

Faithful church planters and ministry leaders are those who love God's inspired Word (2 Tim. 3:16–17; 2 Pet. 1:20–21). They can define orthodox beliefs and defend them (Titus 1:9). They desire to see unbelievers come to know the real gospel and be transformed by it (1 Cor. 15:1–4). They desire to see new churches built on "the faith that was once for all delivered to the saints" (Jude 3), helping God's people to detect error and live out the truth of Scripture (Rom. 16:17; 2 Thess. 2:15). And they long to see the nations saturated with sound doctrine (Matt. 28:18–20). Therefore, being theologically sound and gospel-centered is no small matter. Having theological clarity in one's teaching and leadership is essential.

Clyde Davidson underscores the importance of theology in relationship to mission:

> Theological depth and clarity in missions is the very task Jesus gave to the church. Therefore, deep theological understanding is not an optional add-on for the mature but rather the job of every church and every believer. In his Great Commission in Matthew 28, Jesus gives his disciples the job of teaching all nations to observe all that he commanded (v.20). We see this borne out in the ministry of the apostles as well. When Paul summarizes his ministry among

the Ephesian church in Acts 20:27 he says that he has declared to them the "whole counsel of God." Paul's work as
the evangelist-church-planter par excellence was not just a
bare gospel presentation but rather a deep exposition of all
that God had revealed in Scripture. . . . When Paul summarizes his message to a church he has not visited, he writes
the book of Romans![1]

Indeed, a quick glance through the book of Acts shows the
priority of the Word being taught in the work of church planting
(Acts 11:26; 13:13–52; 16:1; 17:2–3; 18:5; 19:8–10; 20:7).

Theologically Sound

Theology isn't an end in itself. If one loves theology more than
Jesus, he or she has missed the purpose of theology. Good theology will always lead to genuine doxology. Good theology is
"necessary to strengthen the church's worship as well as its tasks
of evangelism, discipleship, teaching, service, and missions."[2]

J.I. Packer helpfully summarizes the work of theology and
highlights its interrelated disciplines:

Theology is first the activity of thinking and speaking about
God (theologizing), and second the product of that activity. . . . As an activity, theology is a cat's cradle of interrelated
though distinct disciplines: elucidating texts (exegesis), syn-
thesizing what they say on the things they deal with (biblical
theology), seeing how the faith was stated in the past (historical theology), formulating it for today (systematic theology),
finding its implications for conduct (ethics), commending and

---

[1] Clyde Davidson, "Why Missionaries Need Theological Precision," *Radical.net*
Original Publication December 7, 2021, https://radical.net/article/why
-missionaries-need-theological-precision/.

[2] Daniel L. Akin, David S. Dockery, and Nathan A. Finn, A *Handbook of Theology* (Nashville: B&H, 2023), 10.

defending it as truth and wisdom (apologetics), defining the Christian task in the world (missiology), stockpiling resources for life in Christ (spirituality) and corporate worship (liturgy), and exploring ministry (practical theology).[3]

As ministry leaders, the work of studying doctrine and articulating it clearly and compellingly in our context is something to which we should always be giving attention. We will need to articulate the faith in accessible ways, remembering that we are called to feed sheep, not giraffes.[4] We will need to apply our theology to hurting people pastorally. And we will need to apply our theology to our own lives. Church planters, like other Christians, will need deep truths in dark moments.

Gospel-Centered

There are many doctrinal points I could address in this chapter, but space is limited. Further, most of you who are reading this are coming from a theological tradition and already have a formulated doctrinal statement (in my case, the BF&M, 2000). What I would like to do is simply encourage you to stay committed to *gospel centrality* in life and ministry.

In parts of the world, particularly in the West, we are trying to reach atheists and agnostics who are quite secular in their thinking and apathetic when it comes to religion. There are many "happy pagans" we're trying to reach. However, in other parts of the world, the problem is not trying to get irreligious people interested in divine things, but rather providing theological clarity for religious people. I have seen all sorts of religious practices around the world today, but sadly, many of them are Christ-less.

My friend Femi Osunnuyi—a church-planting pastor in Lagos, Nigeria—and I have talked about the importance of

---

[3] J.I. Packer, *Concise Theology* (Carol Stream: Tyndale House, 1993), 11–12.
[4] Ibid., 12.

theological clarity a handful of times. In his context, people do believe—it's just that they believe in false teaching! So, he has worked hard at building a church centered on the gospel. At an event, he gave a helpful grid for understanding gospel central- ity, differentiating it from other alternatives.

- **Gospel-Denying Churches.** Various cults and extreme brands of liberalism would fit this category. They deny the essential truths of the gospel, and therefore shouldn't be called a church.
- **Gospel-Redefining Churches.** These churches add to or subtract from the gospel. Examples include the pros- perity gospel and the social gospel, or Jesus + religions (rules, rituals, etc.).
- **Gospel-Assuming Churches.** These churches believe the gospel, but they rarely preach it plainly and deeply. They may not deny substitutionary atonement on a doctrinal statement, but it's not communicated explic- itly and regularly in preaching and discipleship. They're kind of *Christianity lite*. Sermons are filled with self-help ideas, ways to be better parents, how to manage finances, and so on, making it hard to distin- guish their teaching from the wisdom of the age.
- **Gospel-Affirming Churches.** Like the previous group, these churches may adhere to the gospel on paper, but the gospel is viewed solely for the purposes of evan- gelism. As such, it's not communicated directly in gatherings but is reserved for outreach ministries.
- **Gospel-Proclaiming Churches.** These churches are a great improvement. They are known for preaching the gospel every week in gatherings, but the gospel is still primarily viewed as an evangelistic tool. This begs the question: What happens after a person is converted? The critique of this kind of church is that the gospel is

often neglected for the purposes of ongoing discipleship. Instead, what is often emphasized is some kind of moralistic behavior (devoid of grace) and a particular way of thinking about culture, which includes (but isn't limited to) a particular political and social ideology.

- **Gospel-Centered Churches.** These churches preach the gospel explicitly every week, but *not just for the unbeliever.* The gospel subsequently shapes and empowers Christian ethics and the life of the Christian community. When ethics are taken up, the gospel is applied. Marriage is taught by looking at Christ's love for the church (Eph. 5:25); generosity is viewed through the lens of Christ's generosity (2 Cor. 8:9); the call to forgive is rooted in Christ's forgiveness for us (Col. 3:13); hospitality reflects the welcome of Christ (Rom. 15:7). Social ministries like orphan care, widow care, refugee care, and care for the poor are motivated by the grace and mercy we have received from God.

First Corinthians is another great book to consider gospel-centered leadership. In the first few chapters, Paul says he knows nothing but Christ crucified (1 Cor. 1–2). Then, in chapter 15, Paul glories in the resurrection. Between chapters one and fifteen, Paul talks about many subjects (lawsuits, church discipline, sexual ethics, and more), but every topic is viewed through the lens of the good news of what the crucified and risen Christ has done for us, and all that he has for us.

Gospel-centered churches place a value on the grand drama of Scripture, believing that God's Word is like a treasure map that leads to Jesus, the promised Messiah. Prophet, Priest, King, Mediator, Temple, Sacrifice, the second Adam, the Promise to Abraham, the Son of David, the Son of Man, the Son of God, the Servant of the Lord, the Messiah, the King, the Redeemer, the Savior—all of these and more are fulfilled in Jesus (John 5:39, 46;

Luke 4:20–21; 24:27, 44). All the promises of God find their "yes" in Christ (2 Cor. 1:20). Seeing Christ throughout Scripture is vital both for our evangelism and for discipling other Christians. As Christians behold the Savior in Scripture, they will experience glorious transformation (2 Cor. 3:18).

The Wonder of the Biblical Narrative

At the center of the story are the events of Easter. D. A. Carson says, "The whole Bible pivots on one weekend outside of Jerusalem."[5] The message of Easter is the best news in the world! The centrality of this weekend is illustrated by how much focus the gospel writers put on the week of Jesus's Passion. Even the Apostle's Creed jumps straight from Jesus's birth to his suffering, crucifixion, and resurrection, with nothing said about his life. There's a reason we make a big deal about Easter: If these things didn't happen, we should call the whole thing off (1 Cor. 15:12–20). Christ has died, he has risen, and he will come again. A healthy church never loses the wonder of the good news.

While recognizing the beautiful diversity of Scripture, and the diamond-like quality of the gospel, Tim Keller contends, "At the heart of all of the biblical writers' theology is *redemption through substitution*."[6] The story of the Lamb inspires awe and praise. Sam Allberry summarized some of the story like this:

- Genesis 22: a lamb for one man
- Exodus 12: a lamb for a family
- Leviticus 16: a lamb for the nation
- John 1: a lamb for the whole world[7]

---

[5] D. A. Carson, *Scandalous* (Wheaton: Crossway, 2010), 11.

[6] Timothy Keller, *Center Church* (Grand Rapids: Zondervan, 2012), 40 (emphasis added).

[7] Quoted on X (formerly known as Twitter) on March 27, 2020.

When John called Jesus the Lamb of God (John 1:29), he had the Old Testament hopes in view. And how does this theme appear later in Revelation? With redeemed sinners from around the globe singing, "Worthy is the Lamb who was slain, to receive power and wealth and wisdom and might and honor and glory and blessing!" (Rev. 5:12).

The redemptive work of Christ is the fountainhead for every spiritual blessing we have as Christians. It's why we need the Bible. There is a sense in which one can understand that there's a Creator apart from Scripture. Passages like Romans 1:18–25 speak of this *general revelation*. But you can't get from a pinecone to propitiation (creation to the atonement) without *specific revelation* (Scripture)![8] It's this good news that transforms sinners and makes us people of hope and joy.

A church member once approached her pastor and said that she couldn't quite understand how the Bible was a unified story. The wise pastor grabbed an envelope and sketched the storyline of Scripture in the following six symbols.[9]

The Story of Scripture

| Creation | Fall | Promise | Redemption | Mission | New Creation |

One could easily draw this overview on a napkin or teach it to children. The image coming down in *creation* refers to the first two chapters of the Bible, where we read of God creating

---

[8] Credit to my friend Landon Dowden for this illustration.

[9] Christopher J. H. Wright, *Sweeter than Honey: Preaching Christ from the Old Testament* (Carlisle: Langham Preaching Resources, 2015), 18. The graphic here has been slightly adapted from the one in Wright's book.

the world. God also created the whole space-time universe, but the emphasis in Genesis is how God created the world in which *we* live.[10] The X symbol refers to Genesis 3 and symbolizes *the fall*. The effects of sin entering the world are seen immediately in Genesis 4–11. The arrow pointing to the right primarily represents God's *promise* to Abraham. God promised to bless the world through Abraham's family—which happened through Jesus. However, we should remember that the promise is as old as Genesis 3:15, where redemption is promised immediately after the fall. There, God promises to send one (through the woman's offspring) to crush the head of the serpent—which happened through the Messiah. The cross symbol represents the life, ministry, death, resurrection, and ascension of Jesus that we read about in the Gospel narratives. It represents *the good news* of great joy: the good news of what God has done for sinners through Christ. The next arrow pointing to the right includes *the mission* of the church, which begins in the book of Acts and continues through us today. The final arrow coming down represents *Christ's return and the new creation* (Rev. 21–22). There will be no more sin, death, sorrow, tears, or fears, but only God dwelling with his people forever.[11]

Some simplify the storyline of Scripture into four stages (*creation, fall, redemption,* and *new creation*). Others prefer to show the link between the *covenants*—the grand promises God made in the Bible. We read of his covenant with *Noah*, and then with *Abraham*. We also read of God's covenant at *Sinai*, and then with *David*. Finally, we arrive at the *new covenant*, foretold by the prophets and inaugurated by Jesus. Covenants are wonderful ways of showing people that God keeps his promises!

---

[10] Ibid.

[11] Ibid., 20.

We need some kind of outline in our minds to tell the gospel story to people. I also encourage people to read the story of Stephen (Acts 7:1–53) and Paul's sermon at Antioch in Pisidia (Acts 13:16–41) which offer biblical examples of the narration of Scripture. (Keep in mind, though, that these are targeted toward a Jewish audience. Consequently, they do not argue the early part of the story—namely, creation and the fall—but rather begin with Abraham and Israel.)

We should remember the value of being able to retell the story of Scripture for both evangelistic and discipleship purposes. Concerning *evangelism*, the unity of the Bible helps unbelievers understand the whole context of Christianity, rather than just the little controversial bits that many of them know. My wife, Kimberly, was recently chatting with one of her unbelieving friends who said that she had no interest in Christianity but would be willing to read through the whole Bible. Kimberly happily agreed to read through Scripture with her but also suggested that they read a book illustrating the overarching story of Scripture. Books like Craig Bartholomew's and Michael Goheen's *The Drama of Scripture* and Vaughan Roberts's *God's Big Picture* are among the many that do this. For kids (but also for adults!), we recommend Sally Lloyd-Jones's book, *The Jesus Storybook Bible*. Concerning *discipleship*, as Christians discover how themes develop across the biblical narrative and how they find their apex in Christ, they are inspired to worship him and experience ongoing transformation.

God is the ultimate storyteller, and there's no story like the story of salvation found in Scripture. We should read both with a magnifying glass (studying the details of a particular passage) and with a wide-angle lens (considering the passage in view of the larger story).[12] This story leads us to faith in our Messiah, making us people of hope and joy. It's one we need to be able to tell and retell to this broken world.

The Work of Gospelizing People

Jesus's view of the Bible was passed down to the apostles, as is evidenced in various places. For instance, Paul bookends his letter to the Romans with statements about the Old Testament and the Messiah (Rom. 1:1b–3; 16:25–27). In his opening words, he shows us how the gospel has its foundations in the Old Testament, declaring that the gospel is God's good news promised in the Old Testament, centered on Jesus, designed to bring all peoples to the obedience of faith for the sake of Christ's name, and transforming everyone who believes (Rom. 1:1–3). Paul then spends many chapters articulating the gospel to *Christians* before getting to the more practical section of Romans 12–15.

Why does Paul spend so much time on the gospel? It is because the good news is not just about entry into heaven; it also shapes gospel-centered community and drives gospel-centered mission—both very important subjects in this letter. To shape a community of both Jews and gentiles, and have them support his ongoing mission to Spain, Paul spends a lot of time articulating the gospel. In his Romans commentary, New Testament scholar Mike Bird says that Paul is "gospelizing" the believers in Rome.[13] That is, Paul wants every aspect of their lives to be shaped and empowered by the gospel. Likewise, theologically driven church planters and leaders are committed to seeing every aspect of believers' lives shaped and empowered by the gospel.

---

[12] This is an analogy from my friend Bryan Chapell.

[13] Michael F. Bird, *Romans* in *The Story of God Bible Commentary* (Grand Rapids: Zondervan, 2016), 32.

There are at least five reasons why believers and churches should follow Paul's example and keep the gospel front and center.

1. The Gospel Changes Lives

God loves to save sinners—and he does so when the gospel is announced to unbelievers. God loves to sanctify his people—and he does this as the gospel is applied to believers. We used to hear the phrase "life change" a lot in church circles, but how are lives changed? Lives are changed by the Life-Changer, Jesus Christ. To see lives changed, we need to keep the Life-Changer at the heart of everything.

2. The Gospel Leads Us to Worship

The good news changes us from the inside out. When affections change, everything changes. If a person loves Jesus deeply, it will change his or her behavior dramatically. Paul's theology regularly leads him to doxology (Rom. 8:31–39; 11:33–36).

3. The Gospel Lifts Us from Despair

Sin, suffering, and death cause believers to despair. Much of ministry involves counseling those in despair. The gospel lifts us from dark nights of the soul by reminding the saints that God's verdict has already been pronounced over them; that though they're suffering, they're still in the grip of the Father's grace, and that even death can't separate them from the love of Christ.

4. The Gospel Unites Diverse Believers in Community

As already noted, Paul is applying his theology in Romans to build a unified people who are quite diverse, as he does elsewhere (Eph. 2:11–22). Real unity is built as we center on the gospel, and a lot of church fights wouldn't happen if we majored on the gospel rather than on individual preferences.

5. *The Gospel Fuels Our Mission*

It seems that many don't have a passion for the nations precisely because they don't have a gospel worth preaching. When we marinate on the gospel's necessity and glory, we will want to proclaim it far and wide. You commend what you cherish, so as people cherish the gospel, they will naturally and instinctively want to commend Christ to the world.

Conclusion

Christianity is not the only religion in the world to have missionaries and preachers. What makes our mission and our proclamation unique is what we declare—namely, the gospel. This is why theological clarity matters. Faithful church planters around the world declare the good news concerning Jesus Christ to a world in darkness. Christ is central in Scripture, and history is moving toward the day of Christ Jesus. Given these truths, church planters and ministry leaders must stay focused on declaring Jesus as Lord to everyone worldwide and nurturing new believers with the Word of Christ.

Prayer Prompts

- Father, make us people who lead from biblical convictions, who are theologically grounded and gospel-centered in all we do.
- Teach us your Word, open our eyes to behold wonderful things from your law, and fill our hearts with your glorious truth.
- Forgive us, Father, when we deny or disregard your gospel in any area of our lives, and give us grace to apply it generously and accurately in all circumstances.
- Help us to lead our churches to see the glory of your gospel and to teach it to others, discipling them in all your ways.

Reflection Questions

1. Why does theological clarity matter when planting churches? Where might you run amok without doctrinal precision and gospel centrality?
2. We need clarity on what we are starting. What is a local church? How do you form a church that grows in health and maturity?
3. What do you believe regarding church membership? Is it biblical? How would you seek to establish meaningful membership in the life of a new church?
4. How would you use the gospel to disciple a believer who is apathetic toward the church, drowning in marital conflict, raising rebellious children, addicted to pornography, or struggling with depression?

5

Mission

Aspiring church planters can be too pulpit-centric early on. (I say this as a preaching professor who believes deeply in the importance of biblical preaching!) The planter can dream about starting a church service where he can preach but neglect the important work of first planting the gospel in the city through the work of evangelism.

From the beginning of the plant throughout its growth and establishment, the church planter must be committed to reaching outsiders. Effective church planters will model a missional lifestyle. There are various ways this might be done, but I want to highlight two:

1. Ministering with gospel intentionality within one's existing networks
2. Practicing hospitality

These two forms of Christian witness have a historical track record of fruitfulness, and I have seen core teams and churches get excited about evangelism when this vision is set before them. They know they likely won't preach at mass evangelism crusades, and many are not very comfortable doing cold-call evangelism (although both are valid approaches and are not to be despised). But every Christian can live with gospel intentionality and practice kingdom-minded hospitality.

This desire to see unbelievers come to faith in Jesus will naturally lead to *disciple-making*, which can be defined simply as "helping others follow Jesus."[1] The Great Commission, after all, is not to make decisions, but to "make disciples" (Matt. 28:18–20). The last command of Christ should be the first priority for Christians, and this central task involves both *reaching* outsiders and *teaching* new converts. These new converts need a lot of time, teaching, example, care, and accountability. Discipling new believers can't be the work of the church leader alone but should happen within the community of believers.

A wise church planter will think about how to disciple new converts *before* the church is planted. What disciplines will you teach them? What pursuits will you put before them? What resources will you recommend to them? That being said, he will also remain flexible in method or delivery model, as each new believer is unique, and people, in general, can be "messy." Discipleship is not a one-size-fits-all approach.

It's a glorious privilege to see new believers begin to follow Jesus. Let's talk about some ways in which we may have this opportunity more often.

Living with Gospel Intentionality in Our Networks

Everyone has a web of relationships, but we often fail to think about intentionally reaching the people who are right in front of us. Evangelism is often seen as adding "something additional" to our lives, but a missional lifestyle involves identifying people with whom we are already connected and seeking to engage them in a variety of ways.

---

[1] Mark Dever, *Discipling* (Wheaton: Crossway, 2016), 13.

The more secular certain contexts become, the more we must think about reaching people outside the church walls. Most unbelievers have no interest in attending our Sunday church services at Imago Dei. In our Western, post-Christian world, we need more than a cool venue, specialty-roasted coffee, good music, or dynamic preaching to attract non-believers. If any unbelievers *are* present in our worship gatherings, chances are someone befriended and invited them outside the church walls—in shopping centers, workplaces, neighborhoods, recreational spaces, or even family gatherings. In other words, we evangelize those in our networks. Let me share some reasons to emphasize this method of mission.

For starters, network evangelism recognizes the sovereignty of God. When you identify the people in your sphere of influence, you should recognize that God has you where you are for his sovereign purposes. It's no accident who you work with, play with, or shop with. God has us living in this time and place in history, surrounded by image bearers that he has sovereignly put in our path (Acts 17:26–27).

Additionally, network evangelism has a historical precedent. In his book *Cities of God*, sociologist Rodney Stark describes how Christianity became an urban movement and conquered Rome:

> [S]ocial networks are the basic mechanism through which conversion takes place. . . . Most conversions are not produced by professional missionaries conveying a new message, but by rank-and-file members who share their faith with their friends and relatives. . . . The principle that conversions spread through social networks is quite consistent with the fact that the earliest followers of Jesus shared many family ties and long-standing associations. . . . Although the very first Christian converts in the West may

have been by full-time missionaries, the conversion process soon became self-sustaining as new converts accepted the obligation to spread their faith and did so by missionizing their immediate circle of intimates.[2]

"Ordinary members" of the church lived with gospel intentionality among their social networks then, and we need to promote this practice today. It was accomplished through ordinary people empowered by the Spirit. Kenneth Latourette, a noted church historian, said, "The primary change agents in the spread of faith were the men and women who earned their livelihood in some secular manner and spoke their faith to whom they met in this natural fashion."[3]

Moreover, network evangelism promotes steadfastness and patience in evangelism. Often, it takes a long time for an unbeliever to embrace Jesus as Lord. Some methods of evangelism can come across as being numbers-driven rather than people-driven. If you're reaching people in your networks, then you must keep loving them and listening to them.

So, the question that every Christian should ask is, "Who are the people in my networks?" It has been helpful for our church to think within these five categories:

1. Familial Network—people in your family
2. Geographical Network—people in your neighborhood
3. Vocational Network—people at your workplace
4. Recreational Network—people with whom you play or hang
5. Commercial Network—people you see at shops

---

[2] Rodney Stark, *Cities of God* (New York: HarperCollins, 2007), 13–14.
[3] Kenneth Scott Latourette, *A History of the Expansion of Christianity* (New York: Harper & Brothers, 1937), 1:116.

We have encouraged our people to try and identify at least *five people* in each of these networks—or if they are low in one area, to increase the number of people in another network. Then, we have asked them to do one of five tasks.

1. *Pray for the People in Your Networks*

You may be surprised by what will happen if you simply start this! Prayer is not preparation for the work of evangelism; it is part of the work of evangelism. We believe God saves sinners, so we should cry out to him regularly. C.S. Lewis once re-marked, "I have two lists of names in my prayers, those for whose conversions I pray and those for whose conversions I *give thanks*. The little trickle of transferences from List A to List B is a great comfort."[4] A good place to start doing the work of evangelism is by asking the Lord to allow you to see just one person in your network go from list A to list B!

Further, let me encourage you to constantly lead the church to pray corporately for lost people (1 Tim. 2:1–7). Embrace the world in prayer the way the Psalmist does in Psalm 67:1–2:

May God be gracious to us and bless us
     and make his face to shine upon us,   *Selah*
that your way may be known on earth,
     your saving power among all nations.

Notice there's no period after verse one, but a pause (Selah). The people of God are praying for God to bless them so *that* the nations may come to know and worship God. It's a missionary prayer. An evangelistic church asks the Lord to turn unbelievers

---

[4] Philip Ryken, "C.S. Lewis the Evangelist," *cslewisinstitute.org*, Original Pub-lication September 3, 2009, https://www.cslewisinstitute.org/resources /c-s-lewis-the-evangelist/.

(in their neighborhoods and among the nations) into worshipers.

If we believe salvation is of the Lord (Jonah 2:9), then we must pray for God to convert people. We can have the right name, logo, a clean website, acronyms, and strategy, but we don't have anything if we don't have the hand of God upon our lives and ministries. How is it that a spiritually dead person will come to life in your preaching or evangelism? It's not by eloquence but by God's mighty power.

2. Invite Them to Your Home, an Event, or a Bible Study/Church Service

Find a way to spend time with them. Listen to them. Demonstrate kindness and humility (Col. 4:5–6). If you invite them to a Bible study or church service, offer to pick them up or meet them at the door.

3. Serve Them

Look for ways to bless the people whom God has sovereignly put in your path. Surprise them. Take note of things they like and give them a gift. Identify what they need and try to meet that need. Often, it is good works that lead to opportunities to bring the good news.

4. Offer Them Resources

This may be in the form of books, articles, blogs, videos, sermons, or podcasts. Good evangelists are like good fishermen—they know some fish are caught on different kinds of lures. Intelligent unbelievers may be engaged better with more intellectual reading material. Those who commute a lot may prefer podcasts. It's important to fill our toolbox with good gospel options.

5. *Share the Gospel with Them*

Look for opportunities to explain the good news. Don't overcomplicate evangelism. When you have the opportunity, simply tell them how amazing Jesus is. The key here is to enjoy Jesus personally, then you will begin talking about him instinctively. When I go to a great restaurant, I don't need the manager to give me a workbook on how to commend his restaurant to others! I talk about it because I love it. So it is with evangelism; we commend what we cherish.

Regarding the task of sharing the gospel, I find Peter's words very timely for living out a missional lifestyle within our networks:

> Now who is there to harm you if you are zealous for what is good? But even if you should suffer for righteousness' sake, you will be blessed. Have no fear of them, nor be troubled, but in your hearts honor Christ the Lord as holy, always being prepared to make a defense to anyone who asks you for a reason for the hope that is in you; yet do it with gentleness and respect, having a good conscience, so that, when you are slandered, those who revile your good behavior in Christ may be put to shame. For it is better to suffer for doing good, if that should be God's will, than for doing evil. (1 Pet. 3:13-17)

Peter doesn't give us a formula to follow. Rather, he focuses on the heart and life of a faithful witness.[5] He points out that we should always be ready to share the reason for our *hope*.

Christian hope (which involves steady confidence and delight in God's blessings for us now and in the future) is a vital virtue to cultivate, not only for our faithfulness but also for our witness. The word "defense" (3:15) is the Greek word *apologia*, from which we get "apologetics." At one level, this does demand some level of study ("reason" calls for logical thought, and "to be prepared"

---

[5] See my book *Love Your Church* for more on Peter's instructions and our witness (Epsom: The Good Book Company, 2021), 125–26.

implies study). But here Peter is not describing formal, academic apologetics or debating in a public setting. He has an ordinary conversation in mind. For us, that may be at work, in the gym, at the store, or while walking a neighborhood. Peter is urging Christians to be ready to explain why Christ is more precious than anything and why we have hope beyond the grave. Every Christian can do this because all Christians have this hope!

There is a lot of negativity and despair in the world, and unbelievers can often spot this unique hope that shines forth from us. In other words, Peter calls us to live out *an apologetic of hope* among the people God puts in our path.

This hope, then, flows from our adoration of Jesus. This is very important when thinking about mission. To be a good and faithful witness, we need to adore Christ. We need to be filled with hope every day. One of the ways this hope will be communicated is when *we suffer*. We can enter into conversation with unbelievers and tell them about our hope, or we can communicate this hope when *they are suffering*. Often, evangelism looks more like counseling than street preaching. With "gentleness and respect" (3:15), we can share our hope with those with whom we interact.

Practicing Hospitality

Practicing hospitality is a wonderful way to do both mercy ministry and share the hope within us. Recall that *inviting* people is one of the five ways to reach those in your network. This practice also remains a culturally appropriate way to bear witness (in most contexts). What's more, it's a reflection of our God, who has also commanded us (extroverts and introverts alike!) to be hospitable (Rom. 12:13; 1 Pet. 4:9; Lev. 19:33–34). For those aspiring to pastoral leadership, it's also a qualification for an overseer (1 Tim. 3:2; Titus 1:8).[6]

---

[6] See my book *Ordinary* for more on hospitality (Nashville: B&H, 2015).

God the Host

Like most things in the Christian life, we often struggle with motivation. That's why we should regularly think about the hospitality of God. It will increase both our love for others and our willingness to open our homes and our lives to people.

In the garden, God provided a home and made provision for Adam and Eve. In Exodus, God miraculously provided food and water as Israel wandered in the wilderness; he told them to remember his deliverance through a Passover meal. Further, he took them to the "land flowing with milk and honey" (Ex. 3:8). God welcomes, hosts, cares for, provides for, and blesses his people.

Fast forward to the New Testament and we see Jesus constantly eating with people! He is labeled as "a glutton and a drunkard, a friend of tax collectors and sinners" (Luke 7:34). He hangs out with the hated and all sorts of scoundrels—like Levi and Zacchaeus. Lots of ministry was done around the table.

It's also striking to see the early church's practice of hospitality, gathering in homes for worship and ministry (see Acts 2:46; 10:24; 16:13–15, 30–34; 20:20; Rom. 16:1–15; 1 Cor. 16:19).

In the book of Revelation, we see a glorious vision of God's people at the great wedding banquet (19:7) and of God dwelling with his people (Rev. 22). The book ends with an invitation for the thirsty to come to God and be satisfied forever (22:17). What a gracious, hospitable God!

Be a Good Host

Every Christian, especially those who are called to lead by example, should work on the art of Christian hospitality. Let me share some areas I want to grow in personally.

Expand your guest list. Recall Jesus's words:

> He said also to the man who had invited him, "When you give a dinner or a banquet, do not invite your friends or your

brothers or your relatives or rich neighbors, lest they also invite you in return and you be repaid. But when you give a feast, invite the poor, the crippled, the lame, the blind, and you will be blessed, because they cannot repay you. For you will be repaid at the resurrection of the just." (Luke 14:12–14)

Jesus says that when you have a big event, invite those who can't repay you. Invite the marginalized. If you do this, you will be repaid "at the resurrection of the just." Jesus fills ordinary events, like having people over to your home, with eternal significance.

Serve others; don't try to impress them. Hospitality is not about showing off but about welcoming, loving, and caring for others. As I have talked with people about using their homes to do ministry, I have found that many overthink this. You can do hospitality with paper plates and a simple meal.

While you need some space to rest and retreat in your home, avoid thinking that your house is your refuge. We only have one refuge, and that's our great God (Ps. 46:1)! We need to be good stewards of everything the Lord has given us, and one of those things is a home. If you have small living quarters, you can consider other ways to welcome and host, such as by showing people around town or going out for coffee.

Pay attention to what people like or need. Take notice of what they eat, drink, and get excited about. You can make a great connection by surprising people with their favorite items, and it can lead to some great conversations. Pay attention to any need they may have and offer to help. For example, lend a hand with a home project, help them fix their car or some other appliance, or offer to dog sit. This, too, can build relationships. We recently got to know our neighbors simply by collecting their mail and taking out their trash when they went out of town. They came back and showed up with a care package for us.

Consider your context and skills and make a plan. My wife currently hosts a monthly book club at our house for our neighbors. This is not a "Christian book club," but a group of ladies in our neighborhood reading popular books. Perhaps you love cooking and want to host regular dinner parties. You could have a game night and invite neighbors and coworkers over to play. Maybe you can coach a local sports team and get to know kids and families. Alternatively, you could host a kickball game in the park on Saturdays, or even just set up a basketball net and some refreshments. It's amazing how sports attract kids. Densely urban areas will differ from suburban and rural areas. Dangerous areas will differ from safer ones. To think like a missionary means to think about innovative ways of doing ministry well in your context.

Consider practicing hospitality with others. It can often work well if one person hosts and someone else leads the conversation. Introverts and extroverts can unite in faithful hospitality!

Learn to greet people warmly, engage them sincerely, and say goodbye thoughtfully. The greetings and farewells in the New Testament are filled with warmth and meaning (see Acts 20:36; 21:5–6; Rom. 16:16). When someone comes into your home, greet them affectionately. Take their coat. Offer them a refreshment. Give them a place to sit. Don't stay on the couch and yell for them to come inside! As you have a conversation, ask questions about their life. Don't turn everything back on yourself. Put your phone away. When the visit is over, walk your guests to the door or even to their car (or train or bus stop). All these gestures convey value and love, and people remember them.

This is not an exhaustive list, but hopefully a helpful one. We should always keep learning ways to be more faithful in this ancient Christian practice.

Conclusion

Living a missional lifestyle involves living out the Great Commission with everyday gospel intentionality. God has sovereignly put people in our path in our various networks. We have the privilege of praying for them, serving them, inviting them into our homes and churches, offering them resources, and sharing the hope of the gospel with them. One practical way we can have a meaningful ministry with unbelievers is by being hospitable—a practice fueled by God's gracious hospitality. This is a practice we should always be learning more about so we can become more faithful witnesses in our specific context. As we engage unbelievers warmly and wisely, we should be prepared to disciple them faithfully and effectively.

Prayer Prompts

- Holy Father, thank you for the grace you've shown to us in salvation. Fill our hearts with daily gratitude and our mouths with sincere praise for your kindness toward us.
- Help us to think and live like missionaries in our cities and lead our churches to take the gospel into our neighborhoods and among the nations.
- Give us gospel intentionality toward those in our networks and help us to be examples in showing hospitality to them.
- Make us faithful witnesses and fervent intercessors for the lost among us for your name's sake.

Reflection Questions

1. How are you praying for lost people? How are you leading the church to pray for lost people?
2. How are you practicing evangelism? How often do you personally share the gospel with unbelievers? Can you share a recent example of this?
3. Have you been able to appropriately adapt to another cultural context to befriend someone and minister the hope of the gospel to them? Can you share a time when you made the effort to take the gospel across cultural barriers?
4. How has practicing hospitality been a means for you to share the gospel with those God has placed around you?

6

Teaching

A few years ago, I had the privilege of traveling to Berlin for some meetings with church planters from around the world. On our day off, some of us took the train to the historic town of Wittenberg, Germany. From this little town, Martin Luther set the world on fire with his writing, publishing, teaching, and preaching.

There are many wonderful sights to behold in Wittenberg. However, perhaps my favorite spot is not where Luther lived, nor where he nailed the famous *Ninety-five Theses*, but where he frequently preached: St. Mary's Church. I had visited Wittenberg a year before, so I could hardly wait until everyone else got to see where the reformer had proclaimed the gospel for many years. I also wanted them to see the paintings inside the church which artistically portray its various ministries.

The paintings inside are by Lucas Cranach, a famous artist during the Reformation.[1] My favorite is one depicting Luther preaching, which illustrates how we should view both the Scriptures and biblical exposition. It shows Luther *with one finger on the text and one finger pointing to Christ crucified.* And the congregation's eyes are all fixed on *Christ*—not the

---

[1] See Andrew Pettegree, *Brand Luther* (New York: Penguin, 2016), 143–63.

preacher. As church planters and pastoral leaders, we get to carry on this great tradition: to make Jesus, the hero of the Bible, the hero of every sermon.

While the pastoral qualifications for pastors in 1 Timothy 3:1–7 mainly focus on character, one speaks to a particular ability: *the ability to teach* (1 Tim. 3:2; 2 Tim. 2:24; Titus 1:9). This should come as no surprise because at the heart of our faith is the life-changing message of the gospel that must be heralded and taught, announced and explained.

Of course, every Christian is called to make disciples by teaching (Matt. 28:18–20), but pastoral leaders and planters must have particular skills in this area. Paul's words to Titus give us more specifics as to what this means: "He must hold firm to the trustworthy word as taught, so that he may be able to give instruction in sound doctrine and also to rebuke those who contradict it" (Titus 1:9). Notice three ideas here. First, pastors must have a thorough *knowledge* of sound doctrine. They need to be equipped theologically and be committed to their orthodox biblical convictions. Second, they must have the ability to *instruct* the church in sound doctrine, exhorting them to respond appropriately to it. Finally, they must have the ability to *rebuke* those who teach contrary to sound doctrine—to protect the church, and hopefully, to see these false teachers come to the knowledge of the truth.

In 1 Timothy 4:11–16, Paul gives some important exhortations that help provide a comprehensive vision of the teaching ministry. After critiquing the false teacher's message (4:1–5), and after calling Timothy to train for godliness (4:6–10), Paul continues his challenge, saying, "Command and teach these things" (4:11). Here, he is referring to Timothy's task of passing on apostolic doctrine. Paul then highlights various aspects of a faithful teacher's task and his expected lifestyle. In doing so, he underscores the fact that faithful ministers lead with the Word and by example.

Exemplify Your Teaching Personally

Paul urges Timothy to have his life shaped by the gospel, saying, "Let no one despise you for your youth, but set the believers an example in speech, in conduct, in love, in faith, in purity" (4:12). As many church planters are young, this verse is especially important. People were apparently critical of Timothy's youthfulness—he was probably in his thirties.[2]

It's not hard to imagine the kinds of challenges Timothy would have faced. People may have been jealous of his promotion to leadership at a young age. They could have doubted his competency. They might have disrespected him. And it's not hard to imagine how Timothy would have wanted to respond if operating in the flesh: argumentatively, harshly, impatiently. (In other words, the opposite of what Paul tells him to do in 2 Tim. 2:24–25.)

So, how do you respond to criticism as a young minister? Not by hitting social media sites and aggressively blasting away, but by doing something altogether different: setting the believers an example with your life. People will be less likely to despise your youth if they admire your example (1 Pet. 5:3).[3] The way you overcome the challenge of being criticized for your age is with Christlikeness, which includes speech and behavior graces (1 Tim. 4:12). So, guard your tongue (speech). Watch your habits (conduct). Care for all the sheep (love). Show the church what trusting God looks like (faith). And pursue holiness (in purity). Embody your doctrine. Apply your teaching to your own life.

---

[2] George W. Knight III, *The Pastoral Epistles* in The New International Greek Testament Commentary (Grand Rapids: Eerdmans, 1992), 205.

[3] John Stott, *Guard the Truth: The Message of 1 Timothy & Titus* (Lisle: InterVarsity Press, 1996), 120.

Expound the Scriptures Publicly

This is an important verse on many levels: "Until I come, devote yourself to the public reading of Scripture, to exhortation, to teaching" (1 Tim. 4:13). You will show what you believe about the Bible by how you use the Bible, not merely what you say about it. If you want people to be convinced of the Scripture's authority, sufficiency, and Christ-centered focus, then expound the Bible faithfully and point them to Jesus consistently.

Notice also the biblical pattern of the public reading of Scripture (Neh. 8; Luke 4:16–30; Acts 13:13–52). Paul clearly has this pattern in mind here. The earliest description of corporate worship we find in church history is taken from Justin Martyr's *The First Apology*. In defending the practice of Christian worship, he provides a beautiful vision of God's people gathered together:

> On the day called Sunday, all who live in cities or in the country gather together to one place, and the memoirs of the apostles or the writings of the prophets are read, as long as time permits; then, when the reader has finished, the president verbally instructs, and exhorts to the imitation of these good things (emphasis mine).[4]

Notice how Justin's terms "instructs and exhorts" reflect Paul's appeal in 1 Timothy 4:13. This is the historical pattern for us to follow: biblical exposition. We have the responsibility of explaining what God has said in his Word, declaring what God has done in his Son, and applying this message to the hearts of people whether we meet in a house, a park, a school, or a church building.[5]

---

[4] Robert E. Webber, *Ancient-Future Worship* (Grand Rapids: Baker, 2008), 92–93.

[5] Tony Merida, *The Christ-Centered Expositor* (Nashville: B&H, 2016), 16.

Exercise Your Gift Passionately

Paul urges Timothy to use his gifts and immerse himself in the work of teaching: "Do not neglect the gift you have, which was given you by prophecy when the council of elders laid their hands on you. Practice these things, immerse yourself in them, so that all may see your progress" (1 Tim. 4:14–15). Notice that the teaching ministry is both about *God-given ability* (the gift) and *skill development* (progress).

Use your gifts. Paul doesn't state what Timothy's gift is exactly, but from the context, it seems to be related to the ministry of teaching in the church. God gifts people for the ministry to which he calls them (Rom. 12:6–8; 1 Cor. 12; Eph. 4:7–12; 1 Pet. 4:10–11). Like other spiritual gifts, they are for the good of the church, and so we must *use them* to build up the body (Rom. 12:6; 1 Pet. 4:10)! The gift must not be neglected.

Paul mentions some kind of prophetic message that was uttered about Timothy, as well as the elders laying their hands on him (1 Tim. 4:14). This is similar to when Paul and Barnabas were singled out in Acts 13:1–3, and where the laying on of hands is also mentioned. The elders confirmed God's gifting and calling on Timothy. Likewise, aspiring pastors should be commended by pastors who assess their lifestyle and gifting.

As church planters and pastors, we need to always "fan into flame the gift of God" (2 Tim. 1:6) and never neglect what God has given us. Aspiring pastors should seek to discern their giftings, then cultivate their gifts, and eventually use them in leadership with passion.[6]

Let them see your progress. Timothy is urged to be all in: "Practice these things, immerse yourself in them" (1 Tim.

---

[6] John Stott, *Guard the Truth* (Lisle: InterVarsity Press, 1996), 123.

4:15a). It's an excellent charge for us to be wholly devoted to our ministry, avoiding laziness and distraction. Rest? Yes, by all means. But when it's time to do the work, let's get after it.

One thing that should happen the longer you teach is that people should "see your progress" (4:15b). I'm glad this verse is in Scripture because it implies we can improve! People should see progress in our leadership as we become more tender, better listeners, bolder, wiser, and more winsome. They should see our growth in knowledge and our excitement about what we're learning. And they should see progress in our preaching and teaching.

I remember talking with a well-known pastor about a paper I was writing, which focused on giving a detailed analysis of his sermons. When I told him about my project, he said, "Please use recent sermons!" I appreciated that. Even the best can improve.

Examine Your Life and Teaching Persistently

Paul concludes this important passage with a sober exhortation: "Keep a close watch on yourself and on the teaching. Persist in this, for by so doing you will save both yourself and your hearers" (1 Tim. 4:16). This is a summary verse for the preceding points and the entire work of pastoring.

Watch yourself. Paul gave this same word to the Ephesian elders (Acts 20:28). Watching our life involves watching our affections, for we live and speak out of the overflow of our hearts (Prov. 4:23). The way we watch ourselves is by not allowing our passion for Jesus to cool. It involves drinking deeply from the well of the gospel.

As a pastor, I must take care of my heart. I do this by nourishing my soul—reading good books, being in Christian community, cultivating a vibrant prayer life, exercising, and resting well. Since church planting and pastoral ministry are demanding, we must be very disciplined not to be so absorbed in the work that we neglect our spiritual lives.

Watch the teaching. Every pastor must be able to teach and keep this ministry as a top priority. Our teaching should be accurate, clear, and centered on Christ. While not every elder will have the same degree of gifting, all should be able to explain and apply the text to others in a variety of contexts (such as in classes, counseling, or small groups).

Aspiring church planters should consider preparing about four to six months of sermons before launching the church. I set this idea before planters because one of the challenges, in the early days especially, will be fighting for sermon preparation time. While you likely won't have them all one hundred percent finished, you can do the bulk of the interpretive work and prepare fairly detailed notes ahead of time. Once the church is planted, you can add the application needed for your specific context. One might consider preparing a series through a small epistle like Philippians, Ephesians, or Colossians.

Persist in this. This aspect of Paul's exhortation is easily overlooked. Still, it's vitally important because many pastoral leaders who have fallen out of ministry have done so because they failed to give adequate attention to this part of the verse. At one time, they were watching their life and their teaching. But slowly, for various reasons, they stopped doing self-examination. And the results are tragic.

What's at stake in this persistent self-examination? Paul says, "You will save both yourself and your hearers" (1 Tim. 4:16b). We know we cannot save ourselves, for Jesus alone must do that, but Paul is speaking here of Christian endurance. It's the kind of thing he says to the Philippians: "Work out your own salvation with fear and trembling" (Phil. 2:12b). Many people talk about the emotion of conversion, but the New Testament places a greater emphasis on persevering in the faith than it does on one's initial feelings.[7] By perseverance in godliness and by teaching sound doctrine faithfully, Timothy will save his hearers from the dangers of false teaching, which can cause people to make a shipwreck of the faith.

A Method to Consider

In my book, *The Christ-Centered Expositor*, I provide a general overview of what is involved in doing Christ-centered exposition.[8] One of those sections is on methodology, which consists of a five-step process for sermon preparation. At the end of this chapter is a diagram of these steps.[9]

You may think of these steps as blocks of time or days of a week. The methodology is pretty straightforward and is one that I continue to use.

First, study the text. The call to preach is a call to study. As my preaching professor used to say, "If you're going to say, 'Thus sayeth the Lord,' you better know what the Lord sayeth."[10] I love what we read about Ezra: "For Era had set his heart to study the Law of the Lord, and to do it and to teach his statutes and rules in Israel" (Ezra 7:10). Elsewhere, we are told that the hand of the Lord was on Ezra. The hand of the Lord *upon* you and the Word of God *in* you is a powerful

---

[7] Ibid., 124.

[8] I have included a sermon feedback guide based on my book *The Christ-Centered Expositor* as an appendix. This evaluation form summarizes much of the content in the book.

[9] I'm indebted to pastor Kevin Larson for the idea of this visual.

[10] I heard Dr. Jim Shaddix say this many times. I commend all his preaching works to you.

combination. Study the text, working through the various phases: observation, interpretation, integration, and implications. At this point, you just have notes. But you should have a good grasp on the passage and how the gospel can be naturally integrated into your sermon, regardless of what you are preaching.[11]

After immersing yourself in the text, try to identify the main theme of the passage. What is the one major idea conveyed in the text that should drive the sermon? Look for the redemptive thrust of the passage as you think through this and ask: *Why did the original hearers need this passage? Why do my hearers need this passage?* I think about this in two parts:

1. What is the main point of the text (MPT)?
2. What is the main point of the sermon (MPS)? (This will be a present-tense application of the MPT.)

---

[11] Here are ten questions to ask of a passage when trying to connect it to Christ:

   (1) Where does this text stand historically in relation to the Christ?

   (2) Does this text speak directly of Christ?

   (3) [For an Old Testament text] Does the New Testament speak about this subject?

   (4) How do the implications of the gospel make these commands possible?

   (5) Does this text reveal a type of Christ (a person, place, event, or institution that corresponds to and prefigures/foreshadows Christ)?

   (6) Does the passage reveal a biblical theme that points to Christ?

   (7) Does the passage show a promise of God that points to Christ?

   (8) Is the passage predictive of Christ?

   (9) How does this passage show mankind's need for Christ?

   (10) How does this passage reveal the nature of God who provides redemption?

This step is important because it brings both authority and unity to your message. The goal is to preach one sermon, not three or four!

Third, construct an outline that is reflective of the text and suitable for your audience. Remember, your outline should support the MPS. If you believe the sermon has one driving point, the outline should consist of supporting points. It may be helpful to write out your MPS, and then let the language of the MPS drip down into your outline so that the sermon remains a unified whole.

Fourth, add the functional elements: *explanation, application,* and *illustration.* After constructing your outline, write out what needs to be explained. You don't have to explain everything, but only what is necessary. Then, ask yourself why your points are significant for your hearers. You may find it helpful to think through a sermon application grid like the one I constructed for myself, which is placed at the end of this chapter. The goal is to think through various categories and demographics so that you offer some diversity in your application. You won't hit every box, but the grid may keep you from only applying the text to individual Christians or specific groups. It allows you to think contextually and drip the vision of your church into your sermons.[12]

You may choose to use an illustration for each point. Sometimes people ask where I get ideas for illustrations from. Just be observant. A good preacher is always thinking about his task. I have also found that when I think through the application grid, illustrations often come to mind as I consider these various categories.

---

[12] I am indebted to my friend Seth Brown for the grid at the end of the chapter. See also Michael Lawrence's *Biblical Theology* (Wheaton: Crossway, 2010), 184.

Finally, add the introduction and conclusion. Why add the introduction last? You need to know *what* you're introducing before you write an introduction. You will likely have some content for your introduction already, like your MPT and MPS, but you may wish to wait until the previous steps are complete before adding a striking opener. Don't be too rigid on this, however. If an opener comes to you early in the process, grab it and prepare to use it! Just don't start there, or else you may inadvertently force the text to fall in line with your introductory message. In your conclusion, try to recap your message instead of adding new material, consider identifying some takeaways, and most of all, bring the hope of the gospel to bear on your listeners.

Once you start working through a process like this, you will begin to write sermons more instinctively. I like to write my sermons out for clarity, for future usage, and because I typically know when my preparation time is finished based on word count. I also like to write my sermon as early in the week as possible, since the key to good writing is good editing. If you don't have time to edit, you may be taking a rough draft with you to the pulpit. Additionally, if I write it out early in the week, it gives me time to internalize it and preach out of the overflow of my heart, rather than being too tied to my notes. This requires some advanced sermon prep so that on Monday I can sit down and write in one stream of thought.

Conclusion

Faithful, Christ-exalting exposition of Scripture is central to the health and vitality of the church. God has given pastoral leaders a unique ability to teach so that they may instruct, bless, exhort, and protect God's people. While the ability to teach is a gift from God, it is also a skill that church planters/pastors should seek to develop. A faithful shepherd seeks to exemplify his teaching personally, expound the Scriptures publicly, exercise his gift passionately, and examine his life and teaching persistently. Having a reliable methodology to follow is a wise practice for handling the Word faithfully.

Prayer Prompts

- Father, make us skilled teachers and preachers so that our hearers may go out into the world with confidence and clarity in your truth for their lives.
- Help us to exalt Christ as the hero of every sermon, always pointing believers and unbelievers to him as their only hope.
- Bless our churches through the faithful proclamation of your Word, equipping them to be missionaries in their cities.
- Strengthen us to keep a close watch on ourselves and our teaching for the good of our congregations and for your glory.

Reflection Questions

1. What is your preaching philosophy? How do you prepare a sermon? How would you go about preparing a sermon plan for three to six months?
2. Can you think of a time when you were able to rightly discern false doctrine and lovingly rebuke a brother, aligning him with the truth of God's Word (Titus 1:9)?
3. How does seeing a particular text through the lens of the Bible's overarching redemptive narrative help you rightly understand and teach it?
4. Can you demonstrate your ability to teach with one of these difficult and often misappropriated texts: Jeremiah 29:11–13; John 15:1; Romans 8:28; 1 Timothy 2:3–4; Hebrews 6:4–8?

Sermon-process diagram mentioned on page 84.

Step 1

STUDY THE TEXT

Obvious Observations: What does the text say?

Responsible Interpretation: What does the text mean?

Redemptive Integration: How is the gospel related to this text?

Concluding Implications: How does this passage apply to us today?

Step 2

UNIFY THE REDEMPTIVE THEME

Identify the main point of the text (MPT).

Determine the main point of the sermon (MPS).

Add a title that reflects the MPS.

Step 3

OUTLINE THE TEXT

Choose an approach.

Choose your words.

Step 4

DEVELOP THE FUNCTIONAL ELEMENTS

Explanation

Application

Illustration

Step 5

ADD AN INTRODUCTION & CONCLUSION

Adding the introduction

Adding the conclusion

Writing the message and praying over it

Sermon-application grid mentioned on page 86.

		SERMON APPLICATION GRID					
DATE	**TEXT**					**SERMON TITLE**	
PREACHER	**MAIN POINT OF TEXT**					**MAIN POINT OF SERMON**	
	UNIQUE HISTORICAL	JESUS' LIFE & WORK	INDIVIDUAL	GENDER & FAMILY	VOCATION	PUBLIC SPHERE	
TEXTS AND POINTS							

APPLICATION GRID

	SERMON TITLE				
	MAIN POINT OF SERMON				
GENDER & FAMILY	VOCATION	PUBLIC SPHERE	LOCAL CHURCH	UNITY & DIVERSITY	NON-CHRISTIANS

Adapted from Mark Dever's "Application Grid"

7

The Church

It should go without saying that aspiring church planters need to have a good grasp of the doctrine of the church (ecclesiology). You need to know what a church is if you intend to start and lead one!

The Wonder of the Church

"I will be their God, and they will be my people" is a phrase used throughout Scripture (Ex. 6:7; 29:45; Jer. 7:23; Ezek. 36:28; 2 Cor. 6:16), and it magnifies the nature of the redemptive work of our covenant-keeping God, who is committed to having a people for himself. The new covenant people of God are known as the *church*, originating on the Day of Pentecost after Christ's ascension (Acts 2:1–47).

A clear understanding of the church will inspire and focus the work of church planting. It's inspiring for several reasons, not least of which is the fact that Christ founded the church and is building it (Matt.16:18). We're even told that he purchased it with his own blood (Acts 20:28). A good church planter loves what Jesus loves, and Jesus loves the church (Eph. 5:25).[1]

---

[1] A brief survey of Paul's letter to the Ephesians helps us sense the wonder of the church:

There's nothing like the church—a local community of brothers and sisters who have been transformed by Jesus, and who are committed to building up one another. The church is an already-but-not-yet assembly of believers. That is, we experience true salvation now (the "already"), but we await full and final salvation in the future (the "not yet") with all of the redeemed when Christ makes all things new.

As an already-but-not-yet community of believers, we show the world both what our king is like and what the kingdom to come will be like through our values, priorities, ambitions, shared life, and our mission of Word and deed in the world. Envisioned this way, the local church is like a little embassy of the greater kingdom of God, living under the gracious rule of Christ.[2] We are situated outside our homeland as strangers and sojourners (1 Pet. 2:11), where our lives and actions are distinct from others. The outside world should look at us and see something different, asking, "You guys aren't from around here, are you?" "No, we aren't," we may say, "for our citizenship is in heaven" (Phil. 3:20).

Ephesians 1:21–23: The church is the body of Christ, with Christ as the sovereign head of the church.

Ephesians 2:11–22: Paul reminds believers (Jew and gentile) of their prior alienation from God and his people, and what Christ has done through the cross to reconcile them to God *and* one another (2:11–18). Paul calls the church *fellow citizens, members of the household of God*, and *stones in God's temple*, with Jesus being the "chief cornerstone" (2:19–22).

Ephesians 3:10: The apostle tells us that the church—made up of Jew and gentile believers—is making known "the manifold wisdom of God" to "the rulers and authorities in the heavenly places."

Ephesians 3:20–21: Paul prays for God to be glorified "in the church" (3:21).

Ephesians 4:7–16: Paul discusses the unity of the church.

Ephesians 5:25: Paul tells us that Christ "loved the church [his bride] and gave himself up for her."

[2] Tony Merida, *Love Your Church* (Epsom: The Good Book Company, 2021), 17.

When a church plant is established and you gather to sing praises to the Triune God, sit under the Word of God, partake in the Lord's Supper, observe a baptism, have fellowship with fellow saints, and pray together, you are doing more than simply attending a religious meeting. You are part of something different, glorious, and eternal. And all of it is made possible through the saving work of Christ Jesus. By planting churches, we have the privilege of being in on God's sovereign work of gathering believers from all over the world, who are zealous for good works (Titus 2:14).

Describing the Church

Former Major League baseball manager, Leo Durocher, quipped, "Baseball is like church. Many attend, few understand." Indeed, many people don't know what a church is. If you ask the average person on the street, they will probably say something related to a church building. While buildings are important, the church is not to be defined as such.

The term "church" (*ekklēsia*) refers to a "gathering" or an "assembly," but the church is more than a gathering. Mark Dever writes, "The church is the body of people called by God's grace through faith in Christ to glorify him together by serving him in his world."[3] The church is a local community of believers who gather for worship and scatter for witness. They share a life centered on Jesus for the good of one another and the good of the world.

In the New Testament, the word "church" describes various things: a small house church (Rom. 16:5; 1 Cor. 16:19); the church throughout the world (1 Cor. 12:28); the church in an entire city (1 Cor. 1:2; Col. 1:1; 1 Thess. 1:1); the church in an entire region (Acts 9:31). In each case, the community of God's people are referred

---

[3] Mark Dever, "The Doctrine of the Church" in A *Theology for the Church*, edited by Daniel L. Akin (Nashville: B&H, 2007), 768.

to as the church. There are also a variety of metaphors to describe the church which include but are not limited to a family (1 Tim. 5:1–2), the bride of Christ (Eph. 5:32; 2 Cor. 11:2), and a body (1 Cor. 12), with Christ as the head (Eph. 1:22–23; 4:15–16; Col. 2:19).

Further, theologians often distinguish between four senses of the church:

- The universal church: the people of God throughout history—past, present, and future.
- The invisible church: all genuine believers alive on the earth; the church as God sees it.[4]
- The visible church: professing believers alive on the earth; the church as we see it.[5]
- The local church: part of the visible church; in a particular location.

The primary focus of this chapter and book is the final category, the local church.

The Marks of the Church

What distinguishes a Bible study at a coffee shop or a few families singing hymns in a home from a local church? Historically, theologians have highlighted two marks of the church:

1. The right preaching of God's Word.
2. The administration of the sacraments (or "ordinances"): baptism and the Lord's Supper. The second mark also carries with it a connection to church discipline/membership and pastoral oversight.

---

[4] Wayne Grudem, *Systematic Theology* (Grand Rapids: Zondervan, 1994), 855–56.
[5] Ibid.

The right preaching of the gospel is essential. It's not the form of the sermon that's being emphasized but the substance. A church is not a church if false teaching is being taught.

The sacraments serve as membership controls, with baptism being the means for admitting regenerated individuals into the church, and the Lord's Supper being a continual means of grace that also demonstrates one's good standing in the local church.

More could be said about what makes a church a church, but these two marks have been used historically. This is important because although a church plant may look very different in its expression, it should still share these fundamental convictions: the right preaching of the gospel and administering the sacraments.

While there is a good bit of debate around the practice of *church membership*, it's important to remember a few biblical truths. First, church discipline assumes that people in the church are *identifiable* (Matt. 18:15–17). For instance, Paul tells the Corinthian church to "purge the evil person from among you." This idea assumes that some people are in, and some people are out (1 Cor. 5:9–13). Second, the New Testament contains lists of members of a local church, which illustrates that its people were distinguishable and known (1 Tim. 5:9–17). Third, we see in Hebrews 13:17 that overseers must give an account for the people they lead, which means they must know *who* they're accountable for.[6] What's more, the metaphors for the church—stones in a temple, members of a family, citizens of a kingdom, and members of a body—all speak to this concept of membership and belonging.[7]

---

[6] Tony Merida, *Love Your Church* (Epsom: The Good Book Company, 2021), 28.

[7] Thabiti M. Anyabwile, *What Is a Healthy Church Member?* (Wheaton: Crossway, 2008), 97–103.

Shepherding the Church (1 Pet. 5:1–5)

The church flourishes under happy, holy, and humble shepherds. The church suffers under domineering, corrupt, and cowardly leaders. In a time in which we read of scandal after scandal, we need to show the world a different picture of leadership—one that reflects the ministry of the Good Shepherd, Jesus (John 10:1–18).

Church planters should not envision their role apart from the work of pastoring. Even in the early days of your core team gatherings, you will be doing pastoral work. Once the church is established, you will be doing more pastoral work. As the church grows, more pastoral work will be needed.[8]

The good news about shepherding is that we don't have to do it alone. Notice how Peter refers to himself as a "fellow elder" (1 Pet. 5:1). The plurality of elders is normative in the New Testament, and it is practically beneficial as well (Acts 11:30; 14:21–23; 15:2; 20:17; Titus 1:5).

Notice also that Peter calls himself a "fellow elder" even though he was one of the twelve and "a witness to the sufferings of Christ" (1 Pet. 5:1). He didn't distance himself or elevate himself from the other elders, but humbly took his position beside them.

One of the most overlooked words in this passage is "So" (5:1) or "Therefore" in the NASB translation. This word draws our attention back to the previous chapter, which is about suffering and persecution. Think how this famous passage

---

[8] Some models of church planting include a church planter who doesn't intend to pastor the church that he has planted. I certainly have a category for that kind of apostolic church planting, but it does not reflect the majority of the church planters that I coach and train. Most intend to stay and lead the new church plant, at least for a season. For this reason, I want to underscore the importance of pastoral ministry in the work of planting.

about pastoral leadership is written in the context of being afflicted for the sake of the gospel. Peter may be connecting us back to 1 Peter 4:12–19 because, in hostile settings, pastors are often the first to be persecuted. Alternatively, he may be saying that since opposition puts a strain on the community, the need for faithful leadership increases; that is, people need leadership more—not less—in difficult times. In either case, there's no room for self-pity in ministry leadership. We signed up for hardship. Pastors in various places worldwide understand that you enter the ministry with your eyes wide open to the possibility of persecution. Let us never forget this and be prepared to shepherd well when hard times come.

Peter underlines the responsibility of pastors to "shepherd the flock of God that is among you, exercising oversight" (1 Pet. 5:2). In his helpful book, *The Shepherd Leader*, Tim Witmer points out that faithful shepherds have four primary responsibilities: *know the sheep, lead the sheep, protect the sheep,* and *feed the sheep.*[9]

Knowing the sheep. Peter exhorts elders to "shepherd the flock of God that is among you" (1 Pet. 5:2). Previously, he said that Christians should not suffer as a "meddler" (4:15). This word *allotriepiskopos* comes from two root words: *allotrios* ("belonging to another") and *episkopos* ("overseer"). It can be translated to mean something like "one who watches over that which belongs to another." Or to say it another way, it's *pastoring where you don't belong.* If that were a problem in the first century, imagine what Peter would say about those who do this for hours on social media! As leaders of local churches, we should avoid being busybodies and focus on shepherding the church the Lord has allowed us to lead and serve. Know

---

[9] Timothy Z. Witmer, *The Shepherd Leader* (Phillipsburg: P&R, 2010), 189.

your church's macro weaknesses as well as the needs of individuals.

Leading the sheep. To lead God's sheep involves applying the New Testament's vision of the church to one's local context. It means having a clear and executable mission. It involves making wise decisions that build up the entire church. It involves equipping others for ministry and delegating certain responsibilities. It means giving counsel and developing other leaders. And in all of this, it involves setting an example for others to follow (1 Pet. 5:3; Heb. 13:7).

Feeding the sheep. It is fundamental to feed God's sheep, for if sheep don't eat, they won't survive. Expounding Scripture weekly nourishes God's people (1 Pet. 1:23–2:3; John 21:15–19). Feed the sheep as you administer the Lord's Supper, reflecting on the gospel deeply. Feed the sheep in your discipleship courses, small-group ministries, and in your mentoring of others.

Protecting the sheep. Protecting God's sheep is also a responsibility of the elders. "Fierce wolves" exist, so we must be on our guard (Acts 20:28–30). We must warn people publicly about the dangers of false teaching. Further, we protect the sheep by practicing healthy church discipline (Matt. 18:15–20) as we guard the church's purity. Sometimes, church discipline doesn't reach the ultimate step of exclusion (Matt. 18:17) because private warning achieves the purpose of restoring a wayward brother or sister (Matt. 18:15–16; Gal. 6:1).

In a concise manner, Peter tells us how to shepherd: "not under compulsion, but willingly, as God would have you; not for shameful gain, but eagerly; not domineering over those in your charge but being examples to the flock" (1 Pet. 5:2b–3). These are some of the most prominent temptations for pastoral leaders today.

Not out of compulsion, but willingly. No one should have to force someone to be a pastor. This should be something to which a pastor aspires (1 Tim. 3:1). Moreover, we should do our work gladly, not coldly or grudgingly. Whether it's pastoral counseling, sermon preparation, or a staff meeting, let us never lose the wonder of grace, and so do our work happily unto the Lord.

To be sure, there will be times in which we may not be in the best mood! "Willingness" means that we will do our job well even in those times. In season or out of season, the faithful shepherd attends to his sacred responsibilities.

However, if we find ourselves in a prolonged period of drudgery-based duty instead of glad willingness, we need to revisit the gospel afresh. In light of God's mercy and grace toward us, we should stand in awe of the fact that we're in the ministry by the mercy of God (2 Cor. 4:1). It's not that we *have* to attend another elder meeting, or prepare another sermon, or lead the prayer meeting—we *get* to do these things. So, when we feel like the work is overly laborious, we should confess this to the Lord and ask for renewed joy. We should seek out other brothers and sisters for support and encouragement. And we should examine our lives to see if we are making sufficient space for rest and recreation.

Not for shameful gain, but eagerly. One famous baseball player once said that he would play for free simply because he loved the game so much. Many pastoral leaders do ministry with little to no compensation for the sheer love of Christ and the church. However, countless stories could be told about church scandals related to shameful gain. We must guard our hearts against greed (Luke 12:15; 1. Tim 3:3, 6:5; Titus 1:7; 2 Pet. 2:14), and we should also not play favorites with the congregation based on one's financial ability.

If you are an aspiring planter/pastor or a young ministry leader, please keep a close watch on your love for selfish gain as you grow older. The pattern I have observed is that one initially enters ministry out of our sheer love for it, but over time, our hearts can be drawn away to selfish desires. Author and theology professor at Covenant Theological Seminary, Dan Doriani, says, "It's one thing to *make* money, another to *serve* it."[10] We should guard against this drift and be aware of the relentless attacks of the enemy who wants to devour us (1 Pet. 5:8). The devil has a history of using shameful gain as one of his main allurements. Let us cultivate hearts of grace, generosity, and selflessness so that we are not consumed in this way.

Not domineering, but rather setting a humble example. Toxic church environments exist today because of domineering, bully pastors. Such behavior is totally out of line with Jesus's model of servant leadership (Mark 10:42–45). It's not always greed or lust that destroys one's ministry; sometimes, it's power. These ungodly leaders are characterized by being manipulative, overbearing, micromanaging, and hyper-controlling. But this is not the way of Christ! Leadership in the church is not lordship over people. It's about following Jesus and setting people an example to follow.

In a striking parallel reference to ministry leadership, Paul says, "Not that we lord it over your faith, but we work with you for your joy, for you stand firm in your faith" (2 Cor. 1:24). So, Paul's goal was *the believer's joy* (Phil. 1:25). There are ten thousand things we could do for someone, but this is a crystal-clear verse about what we long to see in our kids, our small groups, our church, and our mission—that people may delight in Jesus.

---

[10] Daniel Doriani, 1 *Peter* in *The Reformed Expository Commentary* (Phillipsburg: P&R, 2014), 211.

Love the Church Until You See Jesus

Church planting and pastoral ministry are hard work. Paul's metaphors for ministry include a hard-working farmer, a dedicated soldier, and a disciplined athlete (2 Tim. 2:1–7). So, how can we endure it when people leave our church, when the soil is hard, when the church isn't growing, when we are criticized, when we are attacked, and when we encounter great discouragement? We must keep our eyes on Jesus, "the chief Shepherd," who will reward his faithful servants. When our Lord appears, faithful saints will receive "the unfading crown of glory" (1 Pet. 5:4).

The moment we lose sight of this eschatological vision, we can be overcome with the challenges of ministry. But investing in others is worth it when we keep the big picture in mind: Jesus giving us an *unfading* crown of glory. Never lose the wonder of this reality, dear church planter, pastor, or ministry leader. When you see Jesus on that day, you will not regret having shepherded the flock of God faithfully. May we stay low and dependent on him, as we seek him for grace until that day (1 Pet. 5:5).

Conclusion

We must always see the church from the New Testament perspective. When we do, our understanding of the church is elevated. In addition to maintaining a high view, church planters need to be prepared to shepherd God's people faithfully. Pastors are entrusted with the task of shepherding God's flock as under-shepherds of the Chief Shepherd, Jesus. This work involves knowing, leading, feeding, and protecting the sheep. Peter shows us what kinds of motivations we must avoid and those we must embrace.

Prayer Prompts

- Father, help us to love your church as you do.
- Make us happy, holy, and humble leaders of your people, for their good and for your glory.
- Stir our hearts to gather with fellow saints to seek you and pray for your kingdom activity among us and through us.
- Bless our local churches and use them to engage our cities, make disciples, and plant more churches.

Reflection Questions

1. What is your definition of the church? What are some key scriptural texts that you would use to describe the church?
2. Who leads the church? What does this leadership involve? What key scriptural texts would you use to answer this question?
3. Consider the role of elders, deacons, and the congregation. How do you think the church should be structured, according to Scripture?
4. What is your view of church membership? Explain your answer using Scripture.

8

The Nations

Our church has a lot of young families, and we have something like a child born every twelve days! (We're living up to our name, "Imago Dei"!) We have also had the privilege of sending a number of folks out as church planters and missionaries, both domestically and globally. I have found myself on multiple occasions having serious missional conversations with someone while at the same time trying to interact with one of our wonderful kids vying for my attention. One time, when I was talking to a young single gal preparing to relocate to the Middle East to reach Muslim women, I felt a little guy pulling my arm, saying, "I can do the moonwalk! I can do the moonwalk!" After telling him, "Let me see" (it was really good!), this question popped into my mind: *How can we get this little moonwalker to the mission field?* It will take a lot of discipleship.

We're called to make Jesus's last command our first priority: to make disciples among the nations (Matt. 28:18–20). This involves reaching and teaching people both locally and globally. Church planters and pastors lead the way in this and must equip others to do the same.

I believe every church planter should prioritize global engagement from the early days of the church plant, because as Vance Pitman says, "When God births a church, he has the nations on his heart." Even though the church planter will be focused on *his* city, he should still maintain a global vision, realizing that his church can also shake the nations. Faithful church planters and team members share the missionary heart of the psalmist who says, "Let the nations be glad. . . . Let the peoples praise you, O God; let all the peoples praise you!" (Ps. 67:4a, 5).

The Great Commission

The final chapter of Matthew's Gospel begins with the greatest news and ends with the greatest mission. Matthew links many of the first scenes of the gospel with this last scene, connecting Christmas with Easter. At Jesus's birth, we read that he is called "Immanuel . . . God with us" (1:23). At the end of Matthew, Jesus gives his disciples this promise, "I am with you always" (28:20). At his birth, Jesus is called the king of the Jews (2:2). At the end of the book, we read, "All authority in heaven and on earth has been given to me" (28:18). At Jesus's birth, wise men come from gentile lands to worship him (2:1–12). In the final chapter, the disciples worship him, and Jesus sends them to the nations (28:17–20). It's a wonderful conclusion.

Even though the Great Commission is an often-quoted text, we really can never hear it enough. One pastor shared an anecdote about a widely acclaimed theology professor in Scotland that has stuck with me. He was respected by many and even had several military distinctions. The faculty where he taught had regular chapel services, and occasionally this professor would preach there. But each time, he would preach from the same text: Matthew 28:18–20. This certainly wasn't because he didn't know anything else. Rather, his focus illustrated the vital importance of Jesus's command to his followers.[1] It should remain ever before us.

Of course, this text has had a tremendous impact on many others throughout history, including William Carey, the father of the modern missions movement. Carey's farewell address to his congregation before leaving for India was Matthew 28:16–20. He got the Great Commission, or perhaps we should say, "The Great Commission got him." The question is, *has it gotten us?*

When Jesus says, "Go therefore and make disciples of all nations" (Matt. 28:19), he means all ethnic and language groupings of people (*panta ta ethna*). He has in mind "every tribe and language and people and nation" (Rev. 5:9). Therefore, we should go and disciple all ethnic groups.[2] From Genesis to Revelation we see God's passion for the nations. (For starters, see the following passages: Gen. 12:1–3; Ps. 2:8; 67:1–7, 86:9; 96:3; 117:1; Isa. 60:4; 66:18–19; Matt. 24:14; Luke 24:47; Acts 1:8; Rom. 1:5; Gal. 3:8; Rev. 5:9; 7:9). The faithful Christian will share this passion.

The Central Command: Make Disciples

The all-authoritative king, who is with us always, has given his people the command to make disciples. We cannot negotiate with the king but must submit to his charge. And we can submit to it with *confidence* because he is with us and ruling over all things. We also submit to him with *joy* for who he is, what he has done for us, and all that he has for us.

The one imperative of verse nineteen is to "make disciples." Jesus doesn't say "make decisions" (as important as decisions

---

[1] This story is taken from Sinclair Ferguson in an audio sermon of his that I once heard.

[2] For a great survey of "all nations" in Scripture, see John Piper, *Let the Nations Be Glad* (Grand Rapids: Baker, 2010).

are), but "make disciples." Discipleship begins with a decision to follow Jesus, but the goal is total allegiance to him. The goal is not to make some nominal Christians.

Tied to this imperative are three participles in the original Greek: "going, baptizing, and teaching" (28:19–20) which function like imperatives. The mandate is clear: Make disciples by going, baptizing, and teaching.

Make disciples by going. The church is charged to engage the world. Church planters embody this spirit as they go into rural, suburban, or urban areas to make disciples and establish a healthy, multiplying church.

It has been said that the church is not a cruise ship but a battleship. Nothing is more "all about me" than a cruise ship! But the church of Christ has been sent on a mission with the good news, seeking to reach unbelievers and grow them up into maturity.

Make disciples by baptizing. This has both a reaching and teaching component, as well. As evangelistic church planters, we want to see unbelievers confess, "Jesus is Lord!" We want to instruct them in such a way that they're ready to make a bold declaration to the world, through baptism, that they are followers of Jesus. This is a work of grace. As such, we baptize them in the name of our gracious, Triune God.

It is such a joy to see those whom we've been engaging with the gospel declare their allegiance to Jesus and begin growing in him. We should never lose the wonder of this miracle and constantly keep this mission before our people. Church planting is not about shuffling some disgruntled church members from one church to another church. We must keep our eyes, and our people's eyes, on the harvest field in our context.

Make disciples by teaching. New believers need further teaching, and this takes place primarily through the local church (Acts 2:1–47). The church is a family of learners and teachers. We cannot make disciples apart from teaching. Obviously, as a pastor, you need to be "able to teach" (1 Tim. 3:2), but we must also equip all of God's people to teach others how to follow Christ.

In our mission to make disciples, the point is not simply to transfer information to others. Rather, we want them to "observe" (obeying, keeping, and doing) all that Jesus has commanded (Matt. 28:20). In the words of James, we must show them how to be "doers of the word" (James 1:22). The devil knows the Bible. Our goal is to teach people so that they may be *transformed* into the image of Jesus. We are to teach all that Jesus has commanded with this end in mind: that they may obey Christ faithfully.

Several years ago, I heard a golfing analogy about the three different methods of discipleship. As a church planter and pastor, you have the opportunity to use all your clubs—the woods, the irons, and the putter. You could liken the woods, especially a driver, to preaching in corporate worship. The driver covers a lot of ground. It's big. It's visible. It's very good. You need a good driver.

You could liken your irons to the kind of teaching that requires more dialogue than monologue. This is like a class or a small group. As a pastor, I have opportunities to teach in these settings as well—to our interns, membership classes, and other classes. But there's one club that many pastors don't spend enough time on, and that's the putter. You might liken it to one-on-one discipleship or mentoring. A lot of pastors focus exclusively on their drivers, but they also need to remember what good golfers say: "You drive for show and put for dough."

Please understand that I'm not minimizing preaching; I love it, believe in it, and teach it. We need a good driver. All I'm saying, as a disciple-making pastor, is there are more ways to teach than from the pulpit. Let's use all our clubs! And let's not underestimate the important work of discipleship that others are doing in classes or through one-on-one mentoring. Instead, let's encourage people in this good work.

Christ Is with Us

The call to disciple people is a lifelong task that will be challenging, especially in certain contexts. But the good news is that Jesus promises to be with us every step of the way. The king loves us.

The Great Commission can be summarized in four great "alls." It's great not only because it includes the greatest *authority* ("all authority in heaven and on earth" has been given to Jesus), the greatest *mission field* ("all nations"), and the greatest *curriculum* ("all that" Jesus has "commanded"), but also because it comes with the greatest *assurance*: "I am with you always, to the end of the age," or "for all our days." It is worth giving our lives to this mission.

You probably feel unfit for this assignment, but pause for a minute and consider who preserved the Great Commission for us. Matthew, the tax collector, was a hated, despised, and crooked man. He was like a mafia member, but Jesus transformed him. Jesus told him, "Follow me," and he did! Jesus makes sinners his disciples, who then go and make more disciples.

The Great Witnesses (Acts 1:8)

If you have traveled much around the United States, you have most likely crossed state lines. Usually, I don't think too much about it. But in the book of Acts, we see the gospel crossing great lines of significant boundaries. Traveling from Jerusalem into Samaria was not like going from South Carolina to

Georgia![3] This was a great jump. And from there, the gospel began to spread to the ends of the earth to transform all sorts of people.

Albert Barnes summarizes it powerfully:

> This book contains incontrovertible evidence of the truth of Christianity. It is a record of the early triumphs of Christianity. Within the space of thirty years after the death of Christ, the gospel had been carried to all parts of the civilized, and to no small portion of the uncivilized, world. Its progress and its triumphs were not concealed. Its great transactions were not "done in a corner." It had been preached in the most splendid, powerful, and corrupt cities; churches were already founded in Jerusalem, Antioch, Corinth, Ephesus, Philippi, and at Rome. The gospel had been spread in Arabia, Asia Minor, Greece, Macedonia, Italy, and Africa. It had assailed the strongest existing institutions; it had made its way over the most formidable barriers; it had encountered the most deadly and malignant opposition; it had traveled to the capital [Rome] and had secured such a hold even in the imperial city as to make it certain that it would finally overturn the established religion and seat itself upon the ruins of paganism. Within thirty years, it had settled the point that it would overturn every bloody altar, close every pagan temple, bring under its influence the men of office, rank, and power, and that the banners of faith would soon stream from the palaces of the Caesars.[4]

Thirty years. What might the Lord do with you and your church plant in a thirty-year period?

The book of Acts tells the story of how the ordinary people of God, equipped with the Word of God, empowered by the

---

[3] Sermon illustration idea was gleaned from a sermon I heard by Ralph Davis.

[4] See https://biblehub.com/commentaries/barnes/acts/1.htm.

Spirit of God, and captivated by the Son of God, can accomplish the mission of God. It's all about Spirit-empowered witnesses who testify to the gospel, and it is awe-inspiring. You could study it in the following way:

1. God Empowers His Witnesses in Jerusalem (1:1–8:3).
2. God Scatters His Witnesses to Judea and Samaria (8:4–12:25).
3. God Sends His Witnesses on Missionary Journeys (13:1–21:14).
4. God Delivers His Witnesses to Jerusalem and Rome (21:15–28:31).[5]

We stand in this great tradition! It's a big mission—and one worth giving our lives to.

The Antioch Model

One inspiring church plant that impacted the nations was the church in Antioch (Acts 11:19–30; 13:1–3). It's the one that I want our church to resemble the most.

Luke shows us how the church in Antioch was a launching pad for worldwide missions. It became a base of operation for Paul's missionary journey with Barnabas (Acts 13:1–3; 14:26–27), and subsequently, a base for his journey with Silas (15:35–41; 18:22–23).

What made this church so impactful? What are the ingredients of a missional church? The church was marked by:

1. Effective evangelism (11:19–22)
2. Dynamic discipleship (11:23–26)
3. Mercy ministry (11:27–30)
4. Multi-cultural leadership and membership (13:1)

---

[5] Outline adapted from Patrick Schreiner's commentary: *The Christian Standard Commentary* (Nashville: Holman, 2022).

5.   Spirit-directed, church-supported missionaries (13:2–3)

Regarding this last point, Antioch offers a vision of people being sent out to spread the gospel among the nations. John Stott reminds us of the uniqueness of the trips Paul and his companions took, saying, "All the time the action has been limited to the Palestinian and Syrian mainland. Nobody has yet caught the vision of taking the good news to the nations overseas."[6] But by the Spirit's work, Antioch caught this grand vision.

It seems like the whole church was involved in a time of worship and fasting when the Spirit directed Saul and Barnabas to this new work. The church then blessed and affirmed these men as they sent them off. Notice three transferable lessons regarding this episode.[7]

Worship and expectant prayer fueled the mission. You get the sense this was not simply some special prayer meeting but the normal routine of the church. They were a worshipful and praying community. The fact they were fasting indicates that they were praying with expectancy and deep dependency upon God. Churches that impact the world exalt Jesus passionately and seek him in prayer expectantly! Notice that the story begins with prayer, and then after Barnabas and Saul are selected, they pray again. A world-impacting church is a praying church.

The Spirit and the congregation together affirmed this mission. This story doesn't rely on a "God told me to go to Spain" kind of vision that is totally detached from any reference to the church. But neither does it show us a mechanical decision-making process devoid of prayer and the Spirit that often exists in bureaucratic systems. The Spirit gave the word (however this

---

[6] J. R. W. Stott, *The Message of Acts* (Lisle: InterVarsity Press, 1994), 214–215.

[7] I'm drawing these three points from my commentary *Exalting Jesus in Acts* in *The Christ-Centered Exposition* series (Nashville: B&H, 2017), 165–67.

occurred), and then the congregation affirmed this mission. We see here that missionaries are directed by the Spirit and sent and supported by the church. Ultimately, churches send missionaries and church planters—not boards, organizations, or seminaries. We don't see the mighty apostle ever operating in isolation, apart from community. We see a man directed by the Spirit, united with the church.

The church sent their best on mission. Who is set apart for the missionary journey? It's Saul and Barnabas. It requires an act of faith and sacrifice to give away your key leaders, yet the church does it in obedience to God and for the good of others. Jesus loves churches who think beyond themselves.

We recently sent out a church-planting team to Chapel Hill. The group consisted of twenty-eight members, including two of our key elders. It was hard to say good-bye. We call these "gospel good-byes." Missional churches will experience grief, but it's worth it. We will have all of eternity to fellowship together. Right now, we can make sacrifices for the sake of the mission. Missionary churches must continue to send high-capacity leaders and support their work of evangelism and church planting. In so doing, we will demonstrate—albeit very dimly—the missionary heart of the Father, who sent heaven's best, Jesus Christ, for the good of the nations!

If a church isn't sending, it's ending. This may sound counter-intuitive, but churches that are raising up and sending out missionaries and church planters are usually vibrant churches. One reason for this is that sending and planting constantly keeps the mission in front of people in the sending church. Antioch certainly models this.

A Global Church with a Global God

There are many ways you can prioritize global engagement as a church planter. You can take a trip to an international city and learn how other Christians are engaging their context with the gospel. You can adopt a missionary to support at the beginning of your church plant (we did this when we planted IDC). You can and should constantly give a global vision for disciple-making in your preaching and teaching. And you can lead the church to pray for unreached people groups, for missionaries, and for God's glory to be made known among the nations.

Regarding global prayer, I have never forgotten a story from John Stott. I was just starting out in ministry and beginning to catch a vision for the nations. He was expounding on Paul's call to the church to embrace the world in prayer in 1 Timothy 2:1–7, and he shared this:

> Although Paul uses this cluster of four words [*requests, prayers, intercession,* and *thanksgiving*], they all focus on a single theme, namely that they should *be made for everyone* [1 Tim. 2:1]. This immediately rebukes the narrow parochialism of many churches' prayers. Some years ago I attended public worship in a certain church. The pastor was absent on holiday, and a lay elder led the pastoral prayer. He prayed that the pastor might enjoy a good vacation (which was fine) and that two lady members of the congregation might be healed (which was also fine; we should pray for the sick). But that was all. The intercession can hardly have lasted thirty seconds. I came away saddened, sensing that this church worshipped a little village god of their own devising. There was no recognition of the needs of the world, and no attempt to embrace the world in prayer.[8]

May we never be a village church with a village God. We are a global church with a global God. The God who rules the world

---

[8] J. R. W. Stott, *Guard the Truth: The Message of 1 Timothy & Titus* (Lisle: InterVarsity Press, 1996), 61.

wants his people to embrace the nations with proclamation and prayer.

Conclusion

Church planters should prioritize global engagement from the early days of the church plant. This means making the Great Commission a priority with a vision to go and baptize and teach among the nations. This work can be done in a variety of ways, and we can do it with confidence and joy because Jesus is with us and has authority over all things. The book of Acts gives us an inspiring vision of what it looks like to embrace the nations in mission. The church in Antioch in particular gives us a powerful vision of what a missional church looks like.

Prayer Prompts

- Heavenly Father, help us to lead our churches to pray for unreached people groups, for missionaries, and for your glory to be made known among the nations.
- Help us to prioritize global engagement even as we begin our church plants; give us a zeal for saturating the nations with proclamation and prayer.
- Make our churches missional churches who send out our best to go, baptize, and teach disciples among all nations.
- Teach us to be generous and joyful sending churches as we make your last commandment our first priority.

Reflection Questions

1. With the knowledge that Jesus's last command is to be our first priority (to make disciples of all nations), how would you prioritize this in church planting?
2. Why are maturity and multiplication important in disciple-making? How would you foster both maturity and multiplication in the life of a new church?
3. Consider your efforts to make disciples over the last two years. How have you sought to help present others mature in Christ (Col. 1:28)? Who can you point to as an example of your intentionality in disciple-making?
4. Consider the golf club analogy which illustrates discipling from the pulpit (driver), in small groups (irons), and one-on-one (putter). How would you seek to establish weekly and monthly rhythms in which all your clubs could be used to help others follow Jesus?

9

Practical Leadership

As I was developing the essentials of a faithful and effective church planter, I met with some leading voices on the topic. After discussing my content, it was clear that we needed one more category on practical leadership. By this, I mean *stewarding God's gifts wisely and diligently, and carefully implementing best practices in the work of church planting to see ministry effectiveness and God-glorifying outcomes.*

It is good and right to emphasize theological and personal *faithfulness* in church planting, but we should also give due consideration to ministry *effectiveness*. We need planters who know how to get gospel work done well.

Starting New Gospel Ventures

An effective, wise, hardworking church planter with practical leadership skills is a bit of an *entrepreneur*. Webster defines *entrepreneurial* as "having to do with the creation and development of economic ventures."[1] As a church planter, we're about the creation and development of new gospel ventures (for example, creating evangelistic initiatives, developing discipleship models, and starting new churches).

---

[1] See Merriam-Webster online dictionary at https://www.merriam-webster.com/dictionary/entreprenerurialism.

In the podcast, *How I Built This* (from NPR), host Guy Raz interviews leading entrepreneurs and innovators, digging into the stories behind their companies and movements. I've learned about the backstory of Sub Pop Records, Shake Shack, Fitbit, and Five Guys—just to name a few. It didn't take long to detect that these entrepreneurs have several things in common with church planters.

Church planters with entrepreneurial skills are characterized by their *passion*. This includes being a self-starter. It means being disciplined and diligent. It means being willing to work hard at fundraising.[2]

Additionally, these kinds of church planters are *resourceful*. I often say, "Former drug dealers make good church planters" (emphasis on 'former')! What I mean is that they're streetwise and savvy. They know how to get things done with little resources.

Further, church planters with entrepreneurial skills often display *flexibility and creativity* based on their context and opportunities. They cast a compelling vision, develop clear plans for reaching their specific area, and constantly evaluate their work, learning and making adjustments as they go.

Moreover, like entrepreneurs, church planters *gather people*. They can recruit others to join in the new work, including other leaders who are gifted in ways they aren't. They build trust within their teams. They can also appeal to outsiders in a compelling way.

Finally, these catalytic church planters give *attention to practical details*. These include matters like childcare, security, parking, legal issues, fundraising, handling finances, building needs, details concerning corporate worship, communication,

---

[2] As a resource, see Steve Shadrach, *The God Ask* (Fayetteville: CMM Press, 2013).

and so on. While they usually work with others on many of these issues, they don't let them go unchecked.

If a fruitful church planter was on *How I Built This*, chances are that many of these traits would be mentioned. But the Christian leader understands that behind all our "building" is Jesus's promise to build his church (Matt. 16:18). Christ, our Savior, gives us abilities and opportunities, and strengthens us for his work in the world. So, we can only boast in the Lord as the church grows and bears much fruit (1 Cor. 1:31; 3:6).

Proverbs on Diligence

Wisdom literature in general, and the book of Proverbs in particular, is full of concise, pithy sayings about diligence, industry, and hard work. A life lived to God's glory doesn't just happen. It requires thoughtful study, discipline, and godly ambition. This is a feature of practical leadership.

In Proverbs, we are instructed on the one hand to avoid the sluggard's way of life. The sluggard is characterized by several unflattering traits: *indolence, inactivity, idleness, apathy, helplessness, harmfulness, excuse-making, procrastination, emptiness, and arrogance* (see Prov. 10:26; 13:4; 15:19; 20:4; 21:25–26; 24:30–34; 26:14–16). Sluggards don't plant churches! On the other hand, we are instructed to "consider" the ant in order to be wise (Prov. 6:6–11). Imagine the thought of being taught by a bug! But the ant offers a much better example than the sluggard, illustrating what it looks like to work wisely and diligently and take the initiative in every season.

This emphasis on diligence reflects the opening chapters of Genesis, where work is viewed as a privilege, a responsibility, and a means of expressing God's creativity (Gen. 1–2; Ps. 104:23). While the fall has made all work more difficult (Gen. 3:19; Eccl. 2:18–23), it is still regarded as a gift and as something we must do with diligence. Proverbs expresses this high view of work in various ways: "Whoever works his land will have plenty of bread, but he who follows worthless pursuits lacks sense" (12:11), and "The plans of the diligent lead surely to abundance, but everyone who is hasty comes only to poverty" (21:5).

Church planting is hard work. Paul compares ministry to being a soldier, an athlete, and a farmer (2. Tim 2:1–7). We're not rock stars; we're more like farmers.[3] Paul says elsewhere that leaders should lead with "zeal" (Rom. 12:8). I've read many biographies of prominent entrepreneurs and Christian leaders, and none of them were lazy. We must guard against overwork and burnout. However, what I see today in my context is not the problem of overwork but rather entitlement and lack of diligence.

Ecclesiastes on Toil and Wise Industry

While the writer of Ecclesiastes laments the many difficulties of life, he often speaks of the value of work. We're urged to throw ourselves into the tasks of life with energy and confidence. The "Preacher" (1:1) warns us about the difficulties in toil and the danger of overworking and having the wrong motives (4:4–8). Yet, he states that we can still find enjoyment in our faithful labor (2:24; 3:13; 5:18–20; 8:15; 9:10).

Further, the Preacher also calls us to live by faith in this life, with application given to the merchant's ventures and the farmer (11:1–6). Regarding the merchant, he says, "Cast your bread upon the waters, for you will find it after many days" (11:1). This is an expression that most likely speaks of international trade. Merchants were being urged to send out their goods on seven or eight ships, diversifying their investments because

---

[3] Tony Merida, "Church Planters Are Farmers, Not Rock Stars," *The Gospel Coalition*, Original Publication December 19, 2017, https://www.the gospelcoalition.org/article/church-planters-are-farmers-not-rock-stars/.

some of them were bound to bring back a return: "Give a portion to seven, or even to eight, for you know not what disaster may happen on earth" (11:2). In context, the Preacher is saying to the businessman, "Don't allow the unpredictability of life to make you careless or paralyzed with fear, but live by faith, wisdom, and patience."

Phil Ryken applies the Preacher's words about the merchant to the world of ministry:

> Rather than holding on to what we have, hoarding it all for ourselves—which is the error that the man with one talent made in a parable that Jesus told (Matt. 25:24–28)—God invites us to be venture capitalists for the kingdom of God. . . . It is about having the holy boldness to do seven (or even eight) things to spread the gospel and then waiting for God's ship to come in. Some of the things that we attempt may fail (or at least seem to fail at the time)—some of the ministries we start, for example, or the churches we plant, or the efforts we make to share the good news of the cross and the empty tomb. But we should never stop investing with the gospel in as many places as we can. Whenever we engage in kingdom enterprises, we offer the Holy Spirit something he can and often will use to save people's souls.[4]

Indeed, we want to cast the gospel in as many places as we can, in as many ways as we can, and trust God to bring in the ships. Gospel movements have historically happened not only through the renewal of gospel preaching but also through creative missions, like the use of the printing press, songwriting, various types of evangelism, and contextualized ministries.

---

[4] Philip Graham Ryken, *Ecclesiastes* in *Preaching the Word* (Wheaton: Crossway, 2010), 256.

Martin Luther and the Reformation

Martin Luther was not simply a great theologian and preacher, but he was also a practical leader who knew how to get gospel work done. Specifically, he became a world-class master of mass communication. Noted historian Andrew Pettegree's excellent book, *Brand Luther: 1517, Printing, and the Making of the Reformation*, highlights this often-overlooked aspect of Martin Luther's leadership.

Luther turned his small town into a center of publishing. Through his short pamphlets, written in colloquial German style and illustrated by the artist Lucas Cranach, as well as his use of the printing press, Luther sparked the Reformation. Pettegree notes, "Luther was no distracted intellectual, but a man of great practical skill. . . . He spent his whole life in and out of the print shops, observing and directing. He had very firm views on how books should look . . . [he] understood the aesthetics of the book."[5] He adds, "Luther and his friends used every instrument of communication known to medieval and Renaissance Europe: correspondence, song, word of mouth, painted and printed images."[6]

Note that while Luther recovered the gospel of justification by faith alone, the message needed to be heralded, and he found every way possible to do so. He was not just a theologian; he was someone who possessed cultural awareness, the ability to collaborate with his friends, a deep work ethic, an appreciation of art and music, and some business acumen—especially around the printing press.

Pettegree further comments, "[T]he Reformation could not have occurred as it did without print. Print propelled Martin

---

[5] Andrew Pettegree, *Brand Luther* (New York: Penguin, 2016), 9.
[6] Ibid., 11.

Luther, a man who had published nothing in the first thirty years of his life, to instant celebrity."[7] While this certainly wasn't Luther's goal—nor should it be our desire—his gospel ambition led him to use every possible means of communication available to him.

Finally, Pettegree summarizes, "It is these two stories, the spiritual and theological, and the economic and commercial, that need to be woven together to understand the extraordinary impact of the Reformation. In this way, Wittenberg, the small border town perched on the edge of civilization, would share with Luther the responsibility for igniting one of the great transforming movements of the last millennium."[8] Notice that mighty combination: the spiritual/theology *and* the economic/commercial.

First and foremost, church planters must know the gospel and center everything on it, for it is of "first importance" (1 Cor. 15:3). But such a life-changing message should also move us to use every resource we have and seize every opportunity before us to make it known to everyone. Let us cast our bread on the waters, believing that the Word of God does not return void.

As a planter, you cannot do it all, but you should always consider your capacity, gifts, and opportunities, and seek to put them to kingdom use as good stewards of the Master. This may mean writing, blogging, podcasting, producing great videos, preaching at your church and other venues in the city, training pastors, and helping to plant churches locally and globally. Let us do everything we can to spread the gospel and build up Christ's church.

This is a great time to be a spiritual entrepreneur and start something new, sowing the Word of God in as many ways as we

---

[7] Ibid., 11.
[8] Ibid., 24–25.

can, trusting that he will bring in the ships. Jesus Christ is the Lord of the harvest who is gathering a people for himself. If he used Martin Luther in a backwater town to start the Reformation, what might he do with faithful, creative, innovative stewards today?

Some Practices to Consider

There are many questions and concerns that church planters will need to address along the way. Where should you plant a new church? Are you sure you fit that location sufficiently? Who will you plant the church with? Will you be a bi-vocational or co-vocational church planter (a planter who also works a secular job and never intends to leave it), or will you work full-time as a planter?[9] What's your timetable? Who will be your financial partners? What is your vision of success?

Below are some key considerations and lessons I often share. They are not intended to be comprehensive, but they will hopefully prove helpful. (I encourage church planters to talk to many planters about best practices, so take the best of what I have and be sure to glean from others, too.)

Take the preparation time seriously. For those who are in some kind of church-planting pipeline, let me encourage you to prepare some things in advance. For instance, prepare for *criticism*. This may be one of the most difficult aspects of your ministry. Read on this subject. Talk to other pastors. Memorize key passages. Many church planters have grown up being successful at many things, but when they launch a church, they are shell-shocked that not everyone is a fan of their work—and some folks are even extremely critical of them.

Further, let me encourage you to *prepare messages* in advance. This will help you when you hit the ground. You will need

---

[9] Visit newchurches.com for more resources on this topic.

to spend a lot of your early days with people and engaging the city. Prepare an outline of your exegesis, then add specific applications and illustrations once you know your context better. If you can prepare three to six months' worth—do it.[10] You will be glad you did once your days start filling up with everything else. We encourage our guys to prepare for a series on Philippians since it highlights the gospel, prayer, joy, service, partnership, financial provision, and more—all important themes in a church plant.

In addition, work out your *ecclesiology*.[11] What do you believe about pastors, deacons, ministry teams, children's ministry, and so on? Having this nailed down in advance, will help you in many ways. (Be sure to check out the book list in the appendix for recommended reading.) Begin to work through your *theology of suffering* and how you will apply the Scriptures to suffering people. You will most likely be faced with this immediate need. Read good books on the subject and have key passages in mind.[12] You should also prepare to deal with *conflict* on your team. It usually happens early on. Again, do some homework, and work through a conflict resolution strategy that you can implement if needed.[13]

I would also add that if you have time, prepare some *short responses to controversial questions* that you will likely face. You don't need to reinvent the wheel. Some papers already exist. Be prepared to deal with matters such as race, sexuality, and politics.

---

[10] Refer to chapter six.

[11] Refer to chapter seven.

[12] Paul David Tripp, *Suffering: Gospel Hope When Life Doesn't Make* Sense (Wheaton: Crossway, 2018); Elisabeth Elliot, *Suffering Is Never for Nothing* (Nashville: B&H, 2019).

[13] As a resource, see Tony Merida, *Christ-Centered Conflict Resolution* (Nashville: B&H, 2020).

Plant the church that fits you and your context. Do your research on your specific area. Don't try to copy someone else's model, especially in a different context. Be innovative, unique, and strategic. Don't just exegete Scripture, but exegete *your* city. Think like a missionary. Further, plant a church that reflects your uniqueness and fits you, so that you can lead authentically and passionately. Don't try to plant someone else's church, who has different gifts and is in a different context. Plant the church that *you* can lead intuitively because it is an extension of your theology, philosophy, personality, passions, and gifts.

Remember, Church planting is a team sport. In my opinion, a good church-planting team demonstrates the following: *theological unity* (agreement on the essentials), *philosophical unity* (agreement on how you want to "do" church), *relational harmony* (you enjoy being together), *competency* (each team member gets work done), and *diversity* (which will help to give wise and sensitive pastoral care and will also be attractive to outsiders). I have often said, "Team is more important than location." Here are some of the benefits of working with a core team of leaders:

- It protects you from mistakes you could make as the lone leader.
- It compensates for your weaknesses.
- It makes your job more enjoyable and "doable."
- It guards against sacrificing your family.
- It provides accountability and encouragement. Many planters quit because they have no support system. Others quit because they fall into great sin. A team can help prevent these occurrences.
- It enables you to divide the shepherding responsibilities.
- It allows for a team-teaching model to flourish.[14]

---

[14] See Larry Osborne, *Sticky Teams* (Grand Rapids: Zondervan, 2010).

Consider starting small groups early, not later. We started with a core team, and as the group began to grow, we broke into three smaller groups before we launched our first service. We wanted to instill in people that church is not an event you attend, but a people to whom you belong. Then, when we launched our first public service, we could invite people into one of these three groups to emphasize the importance of community life.

Set clear expectations for potential members. Assuming you will have some kind of membership process, clearly articulate what it means to be a church member. It is a shame that there is usually more expected of a frat member than a church member, so we set clear biblical expectations for potential members including attending a membership class, participating in an interview, and making a commitment to our Church Covenant.

Develop a sustainable and executable plan for the multiplication of leaders. The goal is not to just plant one church but many more. Before planting, I had good intentions to create a pipeline (or process) for leadership development, but I struggled to follow through. When I planted Imago Dei, I made it a commitment, and we put it on the calendar. As a planter/pastor, always be working on your "to-be list" not just your "to-do list." That is, have some leaders you're observing, developing, and eventually deploying (2 Tim. 2:2).

Don't give away leadership too quickly. In a church plant, we often struggle to find other leaders. However, it's imperative to demonstrate patience in the process. If you put the wrong person in a place of leadership—in a small group, for example—it could be very damaging.

Teach and re-teach your people to be missionaries. We try to consistently talk about (and model) network evangelism and hospitality. We regularly talk about the work of evangelism and pray for unbelievers.

Plan to rest and retreat. Trials will exhaust you. Tough conversations will exhaust you. Growth can exhaust you. You will encounter departures, failures, and personal grief. So, take a day off! Plan for some extended rest with vacations and retreats. Work to cultivate good rhythms of work, rest, and play. You need to prepare for a thirty-year run, not just three and a half years. In some settings it will take seven to ten years before you start seeing traction (maybe more!). Make sure you're going at a pace you can sustain.

Conclusion

Church planters need practical leadership skills to start and develop new gospel works. They are marked by characteristics like passion, hard work, and resourcefulness. They can gather people, cast vision, and give attention to practical details. They are flexible and creative as they consider how to engage various contexts with the gospel. They seek to wisely apply best practices to see God-glorifying results. In short, they are faithful stewards of all God has given them, and they make the most of the opportunities before them.

Prayer Prompts

- Father, give us sound strategies for planting impactful mission-focused churches in our specific context.
- May we be motivated by Christ and his kingdom, not by selfish ambition, desire for praise, or other wrong motives.
- Help us to be innovative and resourceful as we seek to spread your gospel in as many ways and in as many places as we can.
- Grant us the grace to be faithful stewards of all you've given us, and to make the most of the opportunities before us for the sake of your kingdom.

Reflection Questions

1. How does the concept of being faithful, creative, and innovative stewards reframe our understanding of spiritual entrepreneurship in church planting?
2. Have you ever started something from nothing? How did you go about it? What did you learn from that experience?
3. How would you describe your Spirit-wrought strategic plan for planting a church?
4. Consider the example of Paul. How would you go about selecting others to form a team in this gospel endeavor? What gifts are you looking for in those you hope to recruit?

Conclusion

The book of Acts is a thrilling and encouraging book to read for any missional Christian as we see the gospel powerfully cross great cultural and geographical lines. It goes from Jerusalem and Judea into Samaria and beyond—into Turkey (Asia Minor), Macedonia, Achaia, Ephesus, Rome, and eventually to the ends of the earth. The gospel advances not just into different regions of the world, but into different segments of society, as well. We see it confronting Roman law courts, Greek philosophers, rural Asian farmers, and government officials. All sorts of people are transformed by the good news.

In Acts, Luke emphasizes the unrelenting progress of the gospel over a thirty-year period. Michael Green comments:

> Three crucial decades in world history. That is all it took. In the years between AD 33 and 64 a new movement was born. In those thirty years it got sufficient growth and credibility to become the largest religion the world has ever seen and to change the lives of hundreds of millions of people. It has spread into every corner of the globe and has more than two billion putative adherents. It has had an indelible impact on civilization, on culture, on education, on medicine, on free-dom and of course on the lives of countless people worldwide. And the seedbed for all this, the time when it

took decisive root, was in these three decades. It all began with a dozen men and a handful of women: and then the Spirit came.[1]

Just thirty years! What might God do in your life should he give you thirty more years? I often tell aspiring church planters, "I want you to prepare for thirty years, not three years," and I have written this book with that goal in mind. I pray that as we grow in these nine essentials, the Lord will be magnified in our lives as we seek to engage cities, make disciples, and plant multiplying churches—continuing the mission started in the book of Acts.

The Road to Philippi

One of my favorite accounts of church planting is the founding of the church in Philippi. On the way back home from our missionary care trip last year, I and some of the other elders decided to stop over for a few days with our wives in the city of Thessaloniki before returning home. On one of those days, we decided to go visit the ruins of the ancient city of Philippi. There's a ton to see including the marketplace, the theatre, and the river where Lydia was likely baptized.

We rented a cheap Volkswagen van called a "caddy" (a basic van with no air conditioning vents or speakers in the back, but it got the job done). Our executive pastor, Matt, drove it, so I called him "Matty the Caddy Daddy." With his Spotify music playing in the background, I began looking at Google Maps, hoping to find some things to see along the way. Sure enough, I found an interesting site off the beaten path, outside of the city of Philippi—the remains of the ancient Roman road, the Via Egnatia. Paul would have taken this

---

[1] Michael Green, *Thirty Years That Changed the World: The Book of Acts for Today* (Grand Rapids: Eerdmans, 2004), 7.

very road from the port of Neapolis (present-day Kavala) to Philippi, which was about a ten-mile walk.

As we stood on this road, we thought of the significance of this walk and all that would eventually transpire on this mission. When Paul and his companions reached Philippi, it was the first time the gospel was preached in Europe. Shortly afterward, the first church in Europe was planted.

Although the geographic distinction between continents was not as prominent at the time, it was still an epoch-making event. Traveling from Asia Minor to Macedonia was a cultural, boundary-crossing event. The gospel would eventually spread throughout Europe, and Europe would become a base for missionary outreach around the world.

Of course, Paul's journey was not as pleasant as our drive with Matty the Caddy Daddy! Paul and his companions wandered around before being led to Troas, after which they eventually sailed by boat across the Aegean through Samothrace to Philippi, where they encountered all sorts of challenges (1 Thess. 2:2). Throughout these trials, however, Jesus displayed his power in this city.

Be Encouraged by the Work in Philippi

In Philippi, Paul and his companions *engaged the city, made disciples,* and *established a vibrant and diverse church.* Paul loved this church, later calling it his "joy and crown" (Phil. 4:1).

We learn lots about church planting from Acts 16. We should *be sobered* by the fact that our work may involve suffering, as it did for this team. But we should also *be encouraged* by the fact that different types of people came to know the Lord Jesus. While there would be many converts during his time in the city

(16:40), Luke records three specific individuals whose transformations were amazing. Consider the following chart.[2]

Individual	Race/Culture	Class	Condition	Ministry Approach
Lydia	Asian	Wealthy	God-fearer	Words
A Tormented Girl	Native Greek	Poor?	Spiritual Turmoil	Deeds
Jailer	Roman	Blue Collar	Practical & Indifferent	Example

From this story, we're reminded that all ethnicities and classes of people can be saved; and that people in all types of spiritual conditions can be saved. Some are really influenced by dialogue, argument, and teaching. Others are moved by deeds of mercy. And some are attracted to Christian example. All of them are saved through responding to the gospel (Rom. 10:14–17).

There may be a Lydia waiting for you to clarify the gospel. As you prayerfully present the good news, pray that the Lord would do what he did for Lydia when he "opened her heart" (Acts 16:14) to the message. You will probably encounter some very troubled individuals as well (those dealing with hurt, abuse, abandonment, or spiritual turmoil). May the Lord use you to show them mercy, hope, and freedom. You'll also encounter blue collar dudes. Perhaps God will lead you to minister to them.

Around ten years later, Paul wrote this letter to this church, urging them to keep focusing on the gospel. He thanks them for

---

[2] Chart developed from Tim Keller's case study on Acts 16 in *Church Planter Manual* (New York: Redeemer, 2002), 102.

their partnership, and he models Christian joy for them as he exults in Christ above all. He reminds them of some of the basics of the faith and addresses the need to be unified.

The Road of Church Planting

Who knows what Paul envisioned when he and his team began that walk from Neapolis to Philippi. But when he arrived, the sovereign Lord used them mightily. Converts were made. Disciples were formed. A church was established. Jesus was exalted as Lord of all.

And who knows what road the sovereign Lord may lead *you* down? Who knows what kind of people you will encounter and lead to Jesus? Wherever he takes you, make sure you prioritize the gospel and glorify the risen Lord. And, in every situation, may your testimony exemplify Paul's words from Philippians 1:21: "For to me to live is Christ, and to die is gain."

Our Sufficiency Is from God

A competency list like the one found in this book can seem overwhelming. You may be led to ask yourself: *Who is sufficient for these things?* (2 Cor. 2:16). The apostle Paul not only raised that question but answered it: "Not that we are sufficient in ourselves to claim anything as coming from us, but our sufficiency is from God, who made us sufficient to be ministers of a new covenant" (2 Cor. 3:5–6a). Paul recognized that his sufficiency—or "competency" (CSB)—came from God. We are not sufficient, but our God is. Left to our own resources, we fall short. But our confidence is in the fact that God's grace and power are enough. Ultimately, it is God who makes us competent. He makes a church planter.

Send Network Church Planter Profile

The following nine topics are intended to serve as a general framework for preparing, assessing, training, coaching, and resourcing church planters.

1. The Heart: Does he walk with God?

    a.   Seeks first the kingdom

    b.   Has a vibrant devotional life

    c.   Lives in Christian community

    d.   Pursues holiness and humility

e. Has good rhythms of hard work and rest

f. Demonstrates desperation for God through prayer, privately and with others

2. Relationships: Is he cultivating healthy relationships?

a. Has a strong marriage and manages his household well (if applicable)

b. Deals with conflict in a Christ-honoring way

c. Values and develops Christian friendships and brotherhood

d. Treats people warmly and honorably

e. Collaborates with other like-minded people to engage the city

f. Participates in the Send Network

3. Calling: Is he confident in his calling?

a. Has a deep compulsion for the work

b. Has a sure sense of God's vocational leading, confirmed by his local church's elders/leaders

c. Seeks the Lord through prayer with others for affirmation of God's calling on his life

d. Is passionate about serving God and deeply aspires to be a planter and minister

e. Sets a godly example for others and has a lifestyle that is above reproach

f. Demonstrates spiritual gifts necessary for the tasks

4. Theology: Is he theologically grounded and gospel-centered?

a. Displays a good knowledge of Scripture

b. Studies to communicate basic doctrines clearly
c. Studies the major questions of the day and seeks to give wise and winsome responses
d. Is humble and charitable when disagreeing with others, especially on non-essential matters
e. Leads from biblical convictions
f. Can communicate the big story of Scripture to others

5. Mission: Does he regularly do the work of evangelism and disciple-making?

a. Has a web of relationships with unbelievers and shares the good news with them
b. Practices hospitality for the purpose of mission
c. Has resources ready to share with unbelievers
d. Is constantly thinking about innovative ways to engage unbelievers wisely and effectively
e. Is making disciples currently
f. Lives as a missionary in his city
g. Leads God's people to pray frequently and fervently for conversions

6. Teaching: Does he handle the Word faithfully?

a. Knows how to explain and apply the Bible skillfully
b. Can speak to both believers and unbelievers from the Word
c. Seeks to grow in the skill of preaching and teaching
d. Can teach the Bible faithfully in small and large settings
e. Understands the centrality of Christ in Scripture, and exalts Christ in every message

f.   Uses the Word to guide corporate prayer when gathered with God's people

7. The Church: Does he love the church?

a.   Studies foundational ecclesiological matters and seeks to implement them wisely in the local church

b.   Seeks to cultivate a rich, life-on-life Christian community within the church

c.   Learns lessons for doing church from others, including those in the global church

d.   Has a plan for and is engaged in the development of future leaders to plant more healthy churches

e.   Has experience shepherding people, giving care, counsel, and encouragement

f.   Leads his church in gathering together to meet with God and pray for one another

8. The Nations: Does he prioritize global engagement?

a.   Builds strategic global partnerships to engage in God's mission and to mobilize the church

b.   Leads the church to join in God's global activity by praying for unreached people and places, missionaries, and God's glory among the nations

c.   Gives generously and strategically to gospel-advancing partners

d.   Participates in global mission trips to gain exposure to and experience in cross-cultural ministry

e.   Sends individuals, teams, and long-term missionaries into cross-cultural ministry

9. **Practical Leadership: Does he have the practical leadership skills needed to plant a church in his desired location?**

    a. Is a good cultural fit in his city
    b. Can cast vision and attract others to the mission
    c. Has the ability to start new initiatives
    d. Has a proven record of leading in other settings
    e. Understands finances and is comfortable raising funds
    f. Is motivated by Christ and his kingdom, not by selfish ambition, desire for praise, or other wrong motives

Recommended Book List for Planters

1. The Heart: Does he walk with God?

Spiritual Disciplines of the Christian Life by Donald S. Whitney

Praying the Bible by Donald S. Whitney

Friendship with the Friend of Sinners: The Remarkable Possibility of Closeness with Christ by Jared C. Wilson

Reset: Living a Grace-Paced Life in a Burnout Culture by David Murray

Prayer: Experiencing Awe and Intimacy with God by Timothy Keller

Confessions by Augustine

The Imperfect Pastor by Zack Eswine

Humility by Andrew Murray

A Short Guide to Spiritual Disciplines: How to Become a Healthy Christian by Mason King

Unburdened: Stop Living for Jesus So Jesus Can Live through You by Vance Pitman

Because We Love Him by Clyde Cranford

They Found the Secret by V. Raymond Edman

Victory in Christ by Charles Trumbull

The Indwelling Life of Christ by Major Ian Thomas

The Complete Green Letters by Miles Stanford

On Being a Servant of God by Warren Wiersbe

2. **Relationships: Is he cultivating healthy relationships?**

Life Together by Dietrich Bonhoeffer

Christ-Centered Conflict Resolution: A Guide for Turbulent Times by Tony Merida

The Meaning of Marriage: Facing the Complexities of Commitment with the Wisdom of God by Timothy Keller

You're Not Crazy: Gospel Sanity for Weary Churches by Ray Ortlund and Sam Allberry

Made for Friendship: The Relationship That Halves Our Sorrows and Doubles Our Joys by Drew Hunter

The Calvary Road by Roy Hession

Enduring Friendship by Bryan Loritts

3. **Calling: Is he confident in his calling?**

Am I Called?: The Summons to Pastoral Ministry by Dave Harvey

Discerning Your Call to Ministry: How to Know For Sure and What to Do About It by Jason K. Allen

Is God Calling Me?: Answering the Question Every Believer Asks by Jeff Iorg

The Path to Being a Pastor: A Guide for the Aspiring by Bobby Jamieson

4. Theology: Is he theologically grounded and gospel-centered?

The Gospel by Ray Ortlund

The Gospel Precisely by Matthew W. Bates

Hearers and Doers: A Pastor's Guide to Making Disciples Through Scripture and Doctrine by Kevin J. Vanhoozer

Biblical Theology in the Life of the Church: A Guide for Ministry by Michael Lawrence

The God Who Is There by D.A. Carson

Christ from Beginning to End: How the Full Story of Scripture Reveals the Full Glory of Christ by Stephen Wellum and Trent Hunter

Gospel Formed by J.A. Medders

Saving the Saved: How Jesus Saves Us from Try-Harder Christianity into Performance-Free Love by Bryan Loritts

You Are a Theologian by J.T. English and Jen Wilkin

A Handbook of Theology by Dr. Daniel L. Akin (Editor), David S. Dockery (Editor), Nathan A. Finn (Editor)

50 Core Truths of the Christian Faith: A Guide to Understanding and Teaching Theology by Gregg R. Allison

Guidebook for Instruction in the Christian Religion by Herman Bavinck

Creeds, Confessions, and Catechisms by Chad Van Dixhoorn

Concise Theology by J.I. Packer

Center Church by Tim Keller (chapters 1–6)

Old Paths, New Power by Daniel Henderson

And the Place was Shaken by John Franklin

5. Mission: Does he regularly do the work of evangelism and disciple-making?

Evangelism in the Early Church by Michael Green

Deep Discipleship: How the Church Can Make Whole Disciples of Jesus by J.T. English

Confronting Christianity: 12 Hard Questions for the World's Largest Religion by Rebecca McLaughlin

The Soul-Winning Church: Six Keys to Fostering a Genuinely Evangelistic Culture by J.A. Medders and Doug Logan

Evangelism: How the Whole Church Speaks of Jesus by Mack Stiles

Making Faith Magnetic by Daniel Strange

On the Block: Developing a Biblical Picture for Missional Engagement by Doug Logan

Center Church by Timothy Keller (chapters 7–18)

The Church of Irresistible Influence by Robert Lewis

Externally Focused Church by Eric Swanson

Once You See It by Jeff Christopherson

Kingdom First by Jeff Christopherson

6.   Teaching: Does he handle the Word faithfully?

The Christ-Centered Expositor: A Field Guide for Word-Driven Disciple Makers by Tony Merida

Lectures to My Students by C.H. Spurgeon edited by Jason K. Allen

How Sermons Work by David Murray

Doctrine that Dances: Bringing Doctrinal Preaching and Teaching to Life by Robert Smith Jr.

On Preaching by H.B. Charles Jr.

Preaching: Communicating Faith in an Age of Skepticism by Timothy Keller

Between Two Worlds: The Challenge of Preaching Today by John Stott

Preaching to a Post-Everything World: Crafting Biblical Sermons That Connect with our Culture by Zack Eswine

Preaching Christ in All of Scripture by Edmund Clowney

Preaching the Whole Bible as Christian Scripture by Graeme Goldsworthy

Preaching for Mission: Developing a Missional Culture in Your Church by Matt Carter

Small Preaching: 25 Little Things You Can Do Now to Make You a Better Preacher by Jonathan Pennington

The Supremacy of God in Preaching by John Piper

7. **The Church: Does he love the church?**

The Church: An Introduction by Greg Allison

On Pastoring: A Short Guide to Living, Leading, and Ministering as a Pastor by H.B. Charles Jr.

Gospel-Driven Ministry: An Introduction to the Calling and Work of a Pastor by Jared C. Wilson

The Care of Souls: Cultivating a Pastor's Heart by Harold L. Senkbeil

40 Questions About Pastoral Ministry by Phil A. Newton

Love Your Church by Tony Merida

The Offensive Church: Breaking the Cycle of Ethnic Disunity by Bryan Loritts

Center Church by Timothy Keller (chapters 19–26)

9 Marks of a Healthy Church by Mark Dever

Workers for Your Joy: The Call of Christ on Christian Leaders by David Mathis

Deacons: How They Serve and Strengthen the Church by Matt Smethurst

Church Elders: How to Shepherd God's People Like Jesus by Jeramie Rinne

8. **The Nations: Does he prioritize global engagement?**

Let The Nations Be Glad!: The Supremacy of God in Missions by John Piper

Missions: How the Local Church Goes Global by Andy Johnson

Mission Affirmed: Recovering the Missionary Motivation of Paul by Elliot Clark

When Missions Shapes the Mission: You and Your Church Can Reach the World by David Horner

The Church on Mission: A Biblical Vision for Transformation Among All People by Craig Ott

40 Questions About the Great Commission by Daniel Akin, Benjamin Merkle, and George Robinson

9. **Practical Leadership: Does he have the practical leadership skills needed to plant a church in his desired location?**

Pastoral Leadership for the Care of Souls by Harold L. Senkbeil and Lucas V. Woodford

H3 Leadership: Be Humble. Stay Hungry. Always Hustle. by Brad Lomenick

The Eight Paradoxes of Great Leadership by Tim Elmore

The Multi-Directional Leader: Responding Wisely to Challenges from Every Side by Trevin Wax

Budgeting for a Healthy Church: Aligning Finances with Biblical Priorities for Ministry by Jamie Dunlop

Brothers, We Are Not Professionals by John Piper

Every Day Matters: A Biblical Approach to Productivity by Brandon D. Crowe

Do More Better: A Practical Guide to Productivity by Tim Challies

Center Church by Timothy Keller (chapters 27–30)

Spiritual Leadership by Henry Blackaby

HD Leader by Derwin Gray

The Treasure Principle by Randy Alcorn

Eight Marks of a Faithful and Joyful Marriage

In a non-exhaustive way, allow me to lay out eight marks of a faithful and joyful marriage, using the acronym FAITHFUL.

F – Friendship

If you are in a covenant marriage, then let me encourage you to have fun together! My bride goes to baseball games with me; I go to musicals with her. I make her pour-over coffee in the morning. We have date nights. I love being married! Underneath this friendship is the foundation of any relationship: trust. The writer of Proverbs 31 speaks of an excellent wife, saying, "The heart of her husband trusts in her" (31:11a). In a good marriage, each spouse trusts the other, which is vital for not only remaining faithful to each other in this covenantal relationship but also for maintaining a joyous friendship. The writer of the book of Ecclesiastes, having talked about how hard life is, bursts out with several things to enjoy in this life including bread, wine, white garments, and oil (9:7–8). Before adding one's toil to this list, he says, "Enjoy life with the wife whom you love" (9:9a).

A – Affection

Fondness and warmth stem from personal touch and nearness and interaction with each other. We must avoid harshness (Col.

3:19) and strive after deep affection for one another. Over time, love can grow cold if each spouse turns inward or selfish. The goal is not to co-exist but to practice empathy, kindness, and comfort toward one another.

I – Intimacy

In Hebrews 13, the author puts money and marriage side by side as important areas in which we can please God (vv.4–5). It's a great reminder that many of our battles will come in the realm of sex and money. If you're married, consider ways to ensure not only financial integrity but also romantic intimacy. Many ministers have fallen in one of these two areas.

T – Teamwork

Church planters, if you're married and in ministry, find ways for your wife to flourish in ministry with you. Avoid compartmentalizing your life so much that there's a great divide between ministry life and family life. While I realize you need special alone time with your bride, seek to do ministry with your wife.

H – Honor

We find the call to honor one another in Scripture. Paul writes, "However, let each one of you love his wife as himself, and let the wife see that she *respects* her husband" (Eph. 5:33, my emphasis). Peter writes, "Likewise, husbands live with your wives in an understanding way, showing honor to the woman as the weaker vessel" (1 Pet. 3:7a). Find ways to honor your spouse regularly. Avoid disrespecting each other in verbal or non-verbal ways. Seek to honor each other in front of others. Elsewhere, Paul says, "Outdo one another in showing honor" (Rom. 12:10b). While he is speaking about the Christian community in general here, his admonition is a good goal for a marriage.

F – Forgiveness

A faithful marriage doesn't mean a perfect marriage. Spouses will fail each other and sin against one another. When that happens, we have the great opportunity to repent and seek forgiveness, and to extend forgiveness. Forgiven people forgive people. Therefore, each spouse should reflect deeply on God's forgiveness in order to reflect his forgiveness to the other (Eph. 4:32). The psalmist said, "If you, O LORD, should mark iniquities, O LORD, who could stand? But with you there is forgiveness, that you may be feared" (Ps. 130:3–4). May we who have been forgiven, more than we even realize, seek to display God's mercy to others, especially our spouses.

U – Understanding

While each spouse should seek to understand the other, Peter directs this point primarily to husbands, whom he urges to live with their wives in an "understanding way" (1 Pet. 3:7). This implies trying to see things through her eyes. It means paying attention to her. It means allowing her to talk. It means learning her likes and dislikes and knowing her fears and cares. Seek to know how she is doing physically, emotionally, spiritually, and relationally. To do all this, you must communicate! A major obstacle to a healthy marriage is a lack of communication, which can lead to a lack of understanding and care.

L – Labor

To love someone is to sacrifice for them. This looks like sacrificing time, schedules, and, sometimes, good ambitions. A healthy marriage takes work. But this service is not a burden when it is motivated by love! Recall how Jacob labored seven years for Rachel, but the writer of Genesis says, "They seemed to him but a few days because of the love he had for her" (29:20). The same is true for our labor in Christ; the labor comes easy when motivated by love for the Savior.

Appendix 4

Sermon Evaluation Form

Speaker _____

Text _____

Title _____

Poor . . . . Excellent

I. **Scripture Reading**
   a. Read with Expression   1 2 3 4 5 6 7
   b. Read with Clarity   1 2 3 4 5 6 7
   Comments:

II. **Introduction**
   a. It incited interest   1 2 3 4 5 6 7
   b. It established relevancy   1 2 3 4 5 6 7
   c. It introduced the MPT   1 2 3 4 5 6 7
   d. It introduced the MPS   1 2 3 4 5 6 7
   e. It contained a redemptive quality
                                    1 2 3 4 5 6 7
   f. It included the preacher's expectations
                                    1 2 3 4 5 6 7
   g. It was not too long   1 2 3 4 5 6 7

What was the opener?

Did the introduction give momentum to the rest of the sermon?

III.   Body

a.   Main headings/points/divisions supported the MPS
1 2 3 4 5 6 7

b.   Main headings/points/divisions were derived from the text   1 2 3 4 5 6 7

c.   Each point contained some if not all of the functional elements   1 2 3 4 5 6 7

d.   Functional elements were used with equality
1 2 3 4 5 6 7

e.   The text was explained well, demonstrating research
1 2 3 4 5 6 7

f.   Illustrations were inspirational and instructional
1 2 3 4 5 6 7

g.   Application was tied to the text
1 2 3 4 5 6 7

h.   Specific and transformative application was given
1 2 3 4 5 6 7

i.   Application was used throughout the sermon
1 2 3 4 5 6 7

j.   The gospel was integrated in the sermon naturally and responsibly   1 2 3 4 5 6 7

What was the most effective element(s) of the expositional items in this sermon?

What was the weakest element(s) of the expositional items in this sermon?

How was Christ exalted in this sermon?

IV. **Conclusion**
Summation
a. Content was summarized clearly
1 2 3 4 5 6 7
b. Summation did not contain new information
1 2 3 4 5 6 7
c. Summation led to the response smoothly
1 2 3 4 5 6 7

How was the content summarized?

Response
d. Speaker was clear on how the hearers should respond 1 2 3 4 5 6 7
e. Response was tied to the MPS 1 2 3 4 5 6 7
f. Hearers were pointed to Christ
1 2 3 4 5 6 7

What type of response was offered?

V. **Delivery and Style**
a. Sermon was clear 1 2 3 4 5 6 7
b. Sermon was not dull 1 2 3 4 5 6 7
c. Passion was demonstrated 1 2 3 4 5 6 7
d. Authenticity was demonstrated
1 2 3 4 5 6 7
e. Eye contact was maintained well throughout the message 1 2 3 4 5 6 7
f. Sermon maintained good pace and momentum
1 2 3 4 5 6 7
g. Humor was appropriate and purposeful
1 2 3 4 5 6 7

h. Communication aids helped not hindered
1 2 3 4 5 6 7

i. Preacher spoke with humble confidence
1 2 3 4 5 6 7

j. Preacher spoke with credibility
1 2 3 4 5 6 7

k. Preacher spoke with pastoral care
1 2 3 4 5 6 7

l. Preacher related well to the audience
1 2 3 4 5 6 7

What was the most effective element(s) of the delivery and style items in this sermon?

What was the weakest element(s) of the delivery and style items in this sermon?

VI.   Overall Comments

Bibliography

Daniel L. Akin, David S. Dockery, and Nathan A. Finn, *A Handbook of Theology* (Nashville: B&H, 2023).

Daniel L. Akin, *A Theology for the Church* (Nashville: B&H, 2007).

Thabiti M. Anyabwile, *What Is a Healthy Church Member?* (Wheaton: Crossway, 2008).

Michael F. Bird, *Romans* in the Story of God Bible Commentary (Grand Rapids: Zondervan, 2016).

D. A. Carson, *Scandalous* (Wheaton: Crossway, 2010).

Tim Chester, *Stott on the Christian Life* (Wheaton: Crossway, 2020).

Clyde Davidson, "Why Missionaries Need Theological Precision." Article online at https://radical.net/article/why-missionaries-need-theological-precision/.

Mark Dever, *Discipling* (Wheaton: Crossway, 2016).

Kevin DeYoung, "The Pastor's Personal Holiness," an article available at https://www.thegospelcoalition.org/blogs/kevin-deyoung/the-pastors-personal-holiness-2/.

Daniel Doriani, *1 Peter* in the Reformed Expository Commentary (Phillipsburg: P&R, 2014).

Elisabeth Elliot, *Suffering Is Never for Nothing* (Nashville: B&H, 2019).

Michael Green, *Thirty Years That Changed the World: The Book of Acts for Today* (Grand Rapids: Eerdmans, 2004).

Wayne Grudem, *Systematic Theology* (Grand Rapids: Zondervan, 1994).

Timothy Keller, *Center Church* (Grand Rapids: Zondervan, 2012).

_____, "The Revolutionary Christian Heart." Article online at https://timothykeller.com/blog/2015/2/6/the -revolutionary-christian-heart.

Timothy Keller and J. Allen Thompson, *Church Planter Manual* (New York: Redeemer, 2002).

George W. Knight III, *The Pastoral Epistles* in The New International Greek Testament Commentary (Grand Rapids: Eerdmans, 1992).

Kenneth Scott Latourette, *A History of the Expansion of Christianity* (New York: Harper & Brothers, 1937).

Michael Lawrence, *Biblical Theology* (Wheaton: Crossway, 2010).

D. Martyn Lloyd-Jones, *Preaching and Preachers* (Grand Rapids: Zondervan, 2012).

Tony Merida, *Christ-Centered Conflict Resolution* (Nashville: B&H, 2020).

_____, "Church Planters Are Farmers, Not Rock Stars." Article online at https://www.thegospelcoalition.org/article/church -planters-are-farmers-not-rock-stars/.

_____, *Exalting Jesus in Acts* in the *Christ-Centered Exposition* series (Nashville: B&H, 2017).

_____, *Love Your Church* (Epsom: The Good Book Company, 2021).

_____, *Ordinary: How to Turn the World Upside Down* (Nashville: B&H, 2015).

_____, *The Christ-Centered Expositor* (Nashville: B&H, 2016).

Fred W. Meuser, *Luther the Preacher* (Minneapolis: Ausberg, 1983).

Paul Miller, *A Praying Life* (Colorado Springs: NavPress, 2009).

Adam Muhtaseb, "The Secret to Church Planting (From a Former Muslim)," an article available at https://www.thegospelcoalition.org/article/secret-church-planting/.

David Murray, *Reset: Living a Grace-Paced Life in a Burnout Culture* (Wheaton: Crossway, 2017).

Larry Osborne, *Sticky Teams* (Grand Rapids: Zondervan, 2010).

J.I. Packer, *Concise Theology* (Carol Stream: Tyndale House, 1993).

Andrew Pettegree, *Brand Luther* (New York: Penguin, 2016).

John Piper, "A Holy Ambition," a sermon available at https://www.desiringgod.org/messages/holy-ambition.

_____, "George Mueller's Strategy for Showing God." Message online at https://www.desiringgod.org/messages/george-muellers-strategy-for-showing-god.

_____, *Let the Nations Be Glad* (Grand Rapids: Baker, 2010).

Philip Graham Ryken, "C.S. Lewis the Evangelist." Article online at https://www.cslewisinstitute.org/resources/c-s-lewis-the-evangelist/.

_____, *Ecclesiastes* in *Preaching the Word* (Wheaton: Crossway, 2010).

Patrick Schreiner, *The Christian Standard Commentary* (Nashville: Holman, 2022).

Tom Schreiner, "Proclaiming the Gospel to the Ends of the Earth," a sermon available at https://cliftonbaptist.org/media/sqc5zh5/proclaiming-the-gospel-to-the-ends-of-the-earth.

Steve Shadrach, *The God Ask* (Fayetteville: CMM Press, 2013).

Charles Spurgeon, *Lectures to My Students* (reprint; Grand Rapids: Zondervan, 1954).

Rodney Stark, *Cities of God* (New York: HarperCollins, 2007).

J. R. W. Stott, *Guard the Truth: The Message of 1 Timothy & Titus* (Lisle: InterVarsity Press, 1996).

_____, *The Message of Acts* (Lisle: InterVarsity Press, 1994).

Paul David Tripp, *Dangerous Calling* (Wheaton: Crossway, 2012).

_____, *Suffering: Gospel Hope When Life Doesn't Make Sense* (Wheaton: Crossway, 2018).

Robert E. Webber, *Ancient-Future Worship* (Grand Rapids: Baker, 2008).

Timothy Z. Witmer, *The Shepherd Leader* (Phillipsburg: P&R, 2010).

Christopher J. H. Wright, *Sweeter than Honey: Preaching Christ from the Old Testament* (Carlisle: Langham Preaching Resources, 2015).

About the Author

Tony Merida is the founding pastor of Imago Dei Church in Raleigh, North Carolina, vice president of Planter Development for Send Network, and a Board member of The Gospel Coalition. He's the author of several books, including *The Christ-Centered Expositor*, *Love Your Church*, and multiple volumes in the *Christ-Centered Exposition Commentary* series. He and his wife, Kimberly, have five children.

About Gospel-Centered Discipleship

You may have noticed that there are a lot of resources available for theological education, church planting, and missional church, but not for discipleship. We noticed too, so we started Gospel-Centered Discipleship to address the need for reliable resources on a whole range of discipleship issues.

When we use the term "gospel-centered," we aren't trying to divide Christians into camps, but to promote a way of following Jesus that is centered on the gospel of grace. While all disciples of Jesus believe the gospel is central to Christianity, we often live as if religious rules or spiritual license actually form the center of discipleship.

Jesus calls us to displace those things and replace them with the gospel. We're meant to apply the benefits of the gospel to our lives every day, not to merely bank on them for a single instance of "being saved." A gospel-centered disciple returns to the gospel over and over again, to receive, apply, and spread God's forgiveness and grace into every aspect of life.

Resources from Gospel-Centered Discipleship

Visit GCDiscipleship.com/books.

If God is my refuge, why does life feel so out of control?

Life's difficulties can overwhelm our sense of God's presence, but we can take comfort in the fact that he is near and full of compassion. *The Art of Stability* is not a how-to manual for floating above the pain of life but rather a path for weary hearts to find their way back to Love. By embarking on this journey, we can discover the safety, love, and resilience that has always been available to us through Jesus.

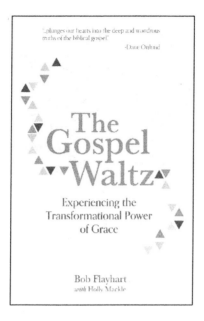

The Christian life involves dance, not drudgery.

The Gospel Waltz is an unapologetic treatise on grace, not shying away from theological truth but processing it through the lens of a simple and highly memorable tool for a life lived abiding in Christ. Through the accessible paradigm of *repent, believe,* and *fight,* the Waltz offers a framework to take hold of the gospel in everyday life and appreciate the transformational and refreshing power of unrelenting grace.

"Develop your leaders . . . or die."

God doesn't want you to plant a church that "needs" its pastor all the time, a church where every answer to every question comes through the church planter. Instead, church planters must develop a community of leaders. *But how?* How do you develop leaders while preparing sermons, fundraising, and finding a new place to meet because you just learned your current meeting location got rented to someone else?

In *Primed to Plant*, seasoned church planter Dwight Bernier explores this topic and many other lessons he's learned the hard way. Whether you're just starting to consider the idea of church planting or whether you're already far enough along to know you need coaching, this book is for you.

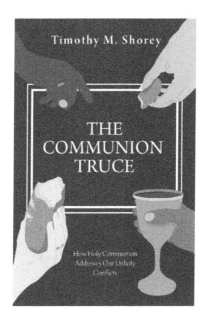

Can't we all just get along?

Christians everywhere recognize the value of Holy Communion as a reminder of what Jesus has done. But author Timothy Shorey believes Jesus intends the meal to do *more* than simply remind. In these divisive and rancorous days—and as we see the Day of the Lord approaching—*The Communion Truce* helps us understand that participating in Communion is not for when every believer gets along and shares everything in common, but for when we don't—so that, by the power of the gospel, we can.

Made in the USA
Monee, IL
03 July 2025

20421362R00108